ENACTING PARTICIPATORY DEVELOPMENT

Theatre-based Techniques

Julie McCarthy with Karla Galvão

London • Sterling, VA

First published by Earthscan in the UK and USA in 2004

ISBN: 1-84407-111-1 paperback
        1-84407-156-1 hardback

Typesetting by MapSet Limited, Gateshead
Printed and bound in the UK by Cromwell Press, Trowbridge
Cover design by Susanne Harris

For a full list of publications please contact:

Earthscan
8–12 Camden High Street
London, NW1 0JH, UK
Tel: +44 (0)20 7387 8558
Fax: +44 (0)20 7387 8998
Email: earthinfo@earthscan.co.uk
Web: **www.earthscan.co.uk**

22883 Quicksilver Drive, Sterling, VA 20166-2012, USA

Earthscan is an imprint of James and James (Science Publishers) Ltd and publishes in association with WWF-UK and the International Institute for Environment and Development

A catalogue record for this book is available from the British Library

Library of Congress Cataloging-in-Publication Data

McCarthy, Julie, 1967–.
    Enacting participatory development : theatre-based techniques / by Julie McCarthy with Karla Galvao.
        p. cm.
    Includes bibliographical references.
    ISBN 1-84407-111-1 (pbk.) – ISBN 1-84407-156-1 (pbk.)
      1. Communication in community development–Developing countries–Problems, exercises, etc. 2.
    Group relations training–Developing countries–Problems, exercises etc. I. Galvao, Karla. II. Title.

    HN981.C6M42 2004
    302.2 09172 4–dc22

                                                                                    2004016780

Printed on elemental chlorine-free paper

CONTENTS

ACKNOWLEDGEMENTS

I am indebted to James Thompson and Viv Gardner for their enduring personal and professional support and encouragement, and to Nicki for her love and patience.

All of the exercises in this book were tested, adapted and in some cases devised by workshop participants in Brazil and Peru. I am extremely grateful for their participation and would like to acknowledge the enormous contribution they have made to this book. I would also like to acknowledge the invaluable support of my friends and colleagues in the UK and apologise to anyone who does not appear in the list below:

Casa de Passagem, Catherine Webb, Clara, Gina and Lucho at Teatro do Milenio, David and Yolanda at Adesa, Dayse Reis, Dida Maia, Elsie Finseth, Enidja Costa, Gilda Souza, Ivete Lourenço, Janayna Lima, Jane Stevens, Jenny Hughes, João Natan da Silva, Josélia Batista Lages, Kátia Pintor, Lúcia Soares, Majê Molê, Marcio André Silva Santos, Marcos Cardoso, Maristela Moraes, Moisés Barreto, Nicki Dupuy, Puchin and Itala at La Restinga, Robert Chambers, Rosana Lucena, Roseane de Oliveira, Silvana Menezes, Suzany Porto, Roberta Kacowicz and Ubiratan Cavalcante.

Karla Galvão was my research assistant on this project. Without her, this book would not have been written.

My final thanks go to Earthscan who have given me the opportunity to bring this book to a wider audience, and to Robert Chambers for encouraging me to do so.

This book is for my daughter, Maia.

FOREWORD

This book comes at a good time. It meets a need. And it is has much to offer to a far wider range of development professionals than just those who already facilitate and use theatre in their work. Let me explain.

Participation in development is not a passing fashion. It has not only come to stay, but it has come to broaden, deepen and evolve. There will always be some who want to say 'been there, done that', or 'tried that, and found it wanting', and look for some new solution. There will always be a few others, methodological fundamentalists, who believe they have the participatory solution and do not look beyond the approaches and methods of one school or orthodoxy. But good development professionals are more pluralist, opportunist, open-minded and eclectic. More and more are now eager for new ideas about how to do better. More and more are trying to lead lives of continuous learning and unlearning. And in doing this they are taking the risks of improvising and experimenting and enjoying the excitement, fulfilment and fun of new approaches and methods. This book is especially for them, and to invite others to join them.

Theatre has been on the margins of participatory development. Closer to the centre have been methods of appraisal and research. These have moved from questionnaires to methods which are rapid, and then to participatory approaches with a host of labels. Visual methods have proved strong and versatile in enabling people to express and analyse their realities. While this has been going on, many have seen theatre as something separate, or to be used didactically to teach people about hygiene, new crops, safe sex and the like. But other traditions of theatre, not least in Latin America, opened up a treasury of opportunities, complementing and enriching other participatory approaches and methods, but still mainly on the fringes.

It is easy to see why even these have remained mainly on the fringes. Many of us (I speak anyway for myself) are shy, inhibited and threatened when it comes to role plays or acting, fearing that we will make fools of ourselves in public and distrusting processes which are so uncontrollable and unpredictable. Many of us are scared to initiate theatre in groups, concerned that things will go wrong, that conflict will arise, that there will be emotions we cannot handle. Many of us anyway have other agendas in participatory processes, and limitations of time. It is easier and safer to stick to what we know and what we know we can do and control.

What we have been missing is the power of theatre and acting for expressing, exploring and experiencing realities. The cerebral activities of development studies, data analysis, policy influence and the like all miss the personal, emotional and experiential dimensions which are fundamental to development as good change. It is as though development has been brain without body or heart. Theatre combines these in a whole which is greater than its parts; it accelerates, deepens and embeds learning and change; and it opens up areas and forms of experiences which are not accessible in other ways.

For those of us who need to overcome inhibitions, and combine head, body and heart, *Enacting Participatory Development* comes to our rescue. The 140 exercises and experiences with them are described in a way which tempts one to try. The objectives are clear, as are the energy level, the time and materials required, and what to do. These are manageable exercises. One can start with some of these and introduce them in the course of training, workshops, fieldwork or meetings. Gaining confidence, the facilitator who wishes can move on then to forum theatre, street theatre or other forms of drama. Nor is this a sourcebook only for newcomers to theatre. There are also ideas and accounts of experiences here for old hands. For all, the exercises are an invitation to be bold and try things out. The case studies illustrate how they can be combined in practice. And the effects of using them are likely to be liberating.

This book is also singularly timely. None too soon, development discourse is recognising the central importance of power and relationships. This applies within groups, as the case studies (pp122–132) illustrate. It also applies within communities and within organisations. It is critical between lenders and donors and those who receive their money, up and down the chains of power and relationships in aid, and between government and NGO organisations and people in communities. The search is on for practical ways in which power relationships can be recognised, analysed, discussed and improved.

The contribution that theatre can make here is enormous. It can enable people, especially those who are 'lowers', or subordinate in a relationship, to explore and express their realities and feelings in ways which are pointed but not personal, and which often provoke laughter. The action and language of puppets and pantomimes, and of forum, street and other theatre, can show and speak truth to power; and power can see and hear, and learn and change. The potential of theatre for empowerment of the weak, and enabling the powerful to change, is little short of phenomenal. So far, though, it remains largely only a potential.

Enacting Participatory Development presents exercises and techniques which can help turn that potential into reality. They can encourage and support shifts in the understanding and practice of power, and empowerment of the weak. If they are well used, not just with groups, but between groups, and between uppers and lowers generally, their effects can be transformative.

So this book is a resource not just for facilitators and trainers who are already into theatre, valuable though it will be for them. It is also an invitation to others to add new exercises and activities to their repertoire, and to enhance the good effects of what they do. For if we are serious about empowerment in development, we have to go beyond rhetoric and words to realities and actions, and beyond the brain to the heart. Theatre has so much to contribute here. And through its theatre-based techniques, this book can do much to encourage and enrich practice. May many trainers, facilitators and others be tempted to try out the exercises. And let me hope that the treasury of practical ideas based on experience which Julie McCarthy and Karla Galvao present will be widely available and used, and that many, many people will have good experiences and better lives as a result.

Robert Chambers
August 2004

INTRODUCTION

Theatre and Development encompasses a growing movement of practitioners, advocates and researchers, who, since the 1970s, have advocated and applied theatre as a tool for participation and social change. One early Theatre and Development practitioner was Ngugi wa Thiongo, who, in the 1970s, was head of the University of Nairobi's literary department and co-ordinator of cultural activities at the Kamiriithu Community Educational and Cultural Centre, Nairobi. As a result of literacy classes at the centre, a series of plays were developed in the local Kikuyu language that made reference to the history of Kamiriithu and the everyday realities of local people through text, dance and song. The reclaiming of the local language, the engagement of local cultural forms and the discussion of everyday life was perceived as such a threat by the Kenyan government, that the Kamiriithu Centre was razed to the ground.

Thirty-five years later, the term 'Theatre and Development' is used to identify a wide range of practice – from scripted plays that disseminate a development message to participatory development initiatives where theatre techniques are used in workshop situations to catalyse action and change.

The scope of academic literature and the availability of practical training courses in this field has expanded rapidly in the last decade. However, access to these valuable resources is generally restricted by geography and economics and there is a paucity of practical manuals, particularly for the development practitioner who wants to incorporate creative techniques into their work but has little or no training in arts-based practice.

In response to the call for more materials, in 1999 I developed the ARTPAD Project which was funded through the UK Department for International Development's (DfID) Innovation Fund. ARTPAD created a Theatre and Development manual written with and for Southern NGO workers who were interested in integrating theatre techniques into their practice, not only in issue-based workshops, but also in areas such as project planning, evaluation, decision-making and research.

The practical sections of the book were developed through participatory research and training workshops held with civil society organisations in Northeast Brazil and Peru, where techniques were created, tested and adapted. The manual has been requested and used by professionals and practitioners in a wide range of development areas including health promotion, evaluation, gender training, participatory budgets, human rights, child rights, reproductive rights and sexual health, rural development, adult education and citizenship.

This book is based on the ARTPAD manual. Some of the techniques included are already well known and documented. Others are new. The exercises are divided into 4 sections: Beginnings; Conflict Resolution; Issue-based Work; and Evaluation. I have also included sections on the theory behind the practical work, case studies, results from our research with NGOs, practitioners and community groups, examples of workshops, a bibliography and a resource section.

In my description of the exercises, I have incorporated comments and suggestions from people who have already experimented with them in the field. These observations are intended to act as a guide for your own workshop planning and to help anticipate any difficulties you might encounter.

I hope that these ingredients will serve as a catalyst for creativity and participation. If you would like to contact me to share your experiences of using this book or other participatory techniques, I would be very pleased to hear from you at: juliemccarthy@onetel.com

HOW TO USE THIS BOOK

This book is not a list of recipes, but a collection of ingredients which I hope you will add to your practice, mix with other ideas and adapt to your needs. Where possible, I have included experiences from practitioners in the field in Brazil and Peru. This will help you to see the possibilities in each exercise and plan how to use and adapt them in your work.

The exercises are divided into 4 sections:

1. Beginnings: warm ups, building a group, working together, focus and concentration.
In these exercises, I address the questions:
How can participants gain awareness of themselves?
How can participants become aware of themselves as part of a group?
How can we facilitate group work?

For example, I look at:
• Ways of developing co-operation
• How to overcome physical barriers to participation whilst respecting personal boundaries
• Ways of ending a workshop.

2. Section 2 focuses on conflict resolution, power and status.
• How can we use theatre to resolve issues within a group?
• How can we use theatre to address issues outside the workshop space?

For example, a number of exercises are included which develop participants' skills in negotiating and problem-solving.

3. Section 3 deals with issue-based work.
• Can theatre-based exercises be adapted for use with any issue?
• Are there specific exercises to deal with specific issues?

During research in Brazil and Peru, exercises were used in workshops on citizenship, sexual health, reproductive rights, gender, human rights, education and the environment. I relate some of these experiences in this section.

4. Evaluation.
Can theatre be used to evaluate?
How can theatre-based techniques be used by participants to evaluate development projects?

All the exercises in this manual have been tested by NGO workers in Peru and Brazil. I have incorporated as many adaptations and experiences from development workers as space and time has allowed.

INFORMATION PROVIDED WITH EACH EXERCISE – A KEY TO USE

45	Each exercise is numbered to make cross referencing easier.
SOURCE	Where appropriate I have provided a source reference for each exercise. Where the exercise is in the public domain or has been developed during the course of the project, a source reference is not given. Full references can be found for source publications in the **Bibliography** section.
OBJECTIVES	What is the main purpose of the exercise? These objectives are not rigid, but give basic guidance on the aims of this type of exercise.
FOCUS	How much focus is on individual participants involved in an exercise? Imagine a light on a stage. If the light is illuminating the whole stage, then the audience will be able to see all the actors and won't be looking at just one person. This is low focus. If the light is falling on just one actor, then everyone will be looking at her, so this is high focus. Low-focus exercises are useful when participants do not know each other very well. High-focus exercises can only be used when a group has developed a sense of trust and intimacy.
ENERGY	This gives an idea of the level of energy needed for the exercise, also, how much energy the exercise generates. A high energy exercise might be needed to revitalise a group after lunch, but would not be appropriate if you wanted to invoke calm and concentration. It is important to look at the overall structure of a workshop and vary the pace and energy levels.
NUMBERS	This gives the minimum number of people you need to do an exercise. This is a guide – you may be able to think of adaptations if you are working with fewer people.
DURATION	This indicates how long you can expect the exercise to take and varies depending on the number of people you are working with and on the group's rhythm. I found that in the Peruvian Andes exercises generally take longer than in Lima where people are in much more of a hurry!
MATERIAL	I have tried to keep these to a minimum. You should be able to plan a whole workshop without using more than pens, paper and a lot of creativity.

PLANNING A WORKSHOP

A good workshop enhances or maintains the physical and emotional safety of the participants and keeps them engaged through a planned and balanced structure.

STRUCTURE

When planning, it is helpful to think of your workshop structure in 3 stages.

* Stage 1 brings the participants together and develops their identity as a group, thus preparing them for the tasks ahead.
* In stage 2, the theme you have agreed to work on is addressed through a planned series of exercises to explore and create material relevant to their own lives.
* In the third stage, the group prepares to leave the workshop. This is done with exercises which, depending on the mood of the workshop, may bring the level of energy back down or provide a chance to release energy and laughter (particularly after working intensely on a challenging subject). This is a de-briefing period which helps participants to rebalance their emotional energy and aims to reinforce their sense of belonging to the group. Ideally, at the end of the workshop, individuals should feel able to separate from the group and have the capability to retain and relate the experiences they have shared to their own lives.

WARMING UP

* If the group has never worked together before, or if there is a new member, participants need to break the ice and get to know one another. Conventional introductions (presenting people to each other using their name and perhaps other information such as their job) maintain status within the group (boss over worker, teacher over peasant farmer) and do not help to break down social barriers. We therefore have to find ways of allowing the group members to see each other as individuals with personal strengths, rather than define them through their status outside the group.

* Groups usually contain sub-groups based on status and interests and each of these sub-groups may also contain its own power structure. Imagine, for example, an organisation carrying out an evaluation session in which the director, project workers and administration workers are participating.

* We should observe how gender relations are expressed in the group, for example, are the opinions of the women given as much value and space as those of the men?

* Ice-breaking exercises shouldn't be threatening to the individual or leave them vulnerable or emotionally exposed within the group, so low-focus exercises are the most appropriate. However, the exercises should provide an opportunity for participants to express themselves as individuals and to give and receive impressions of each other.

* These exercises set the mood for the rest of the session, they are the first impression participants have of you and the workshop, so they should be active and fun. Get people up and doing things, not just sitting around talking.

WARM UPS FOR ESTABLISHED GROUPS

* A group that has been working together for some time still has to warm up for the work ahead.

* Warm-up exercises should focus the attention of the participants on how they are feeling, both physically and emotionally. Do they have any aches and pains? Are they angry? Tired? Tense?

* Warm ups help participants to forget about their shopping lists, the fight they just had with their boss, the field of corn that needs harvesting … they can pick up these thoughts again as they leave the workshop or address their concerns in the group as part of the workshop.

ENERGY LEVELS

* When you are planning a workshop it is vital that you consider the energy level of participants as they arrive and the energy level of participants throughout the session.

* At the beginning of the session, we need to energise the group, as they may have been working all day, perhaps sitting at a computer screen or labouring in the fields. This is why it is important to start DOING as quickly as possible. Don't sit around talking about what you are going to do for 30 minutes.

* Begin with an activity which will stimulate and focus the group. Then, if you need to, you can sit down and talk.

* It is important to tell the group what you are planning to do in the session; they need to know why they are there and cannot be expected to strive towards a goal of which they are ignorant. Starting with action straight away will also help participants overcome any anxiety they may have about participating in the workshop.

* Keep an eye on energy levels all through the session. If you feel that the group is tired, you might want to stimulate them with a high-energy game, or provide a chance for a quieter, more relaxing exercise. If you have been dealing with challenging material with the group, give them the chance to let off steam by playing an energetic game.

HOW DOES A ROOM OF INDIVIDUALS BECOME A GROUP?

* This is a long and sometimes difficult process, even with people who have been working together for some time. I regard this as a cumulative process which has to be focused on heavily in the first few sessions and then built on throughout the workshop process.

* This book contains a large selection of exercises aimed at group integration, one of the keys to successful project work. Participatory development projects do not function effectively unless participants can work well together.

* Games and exercises often reveal power relationships and hidden conflicts between sub-groups or individuals. You may feel that your original aims need to be changed if this happens. Don't worry if you find yourself having to abandon your original plan to deal with these issues. You may have to spend the majority of your allocated time working on conflict within the group, but if you don't build a solid base for work with the group, it will be almost impossible to achieve any other objectives.

* You might also decide to re-plan your session as a result of material generated in a simple warm-up exercise. If the exercise reveals the hidden themes or current concerns of the group, there is no reason not to adapt your original idea to accommodate the concerns of the group. A plan is only a theoretical document. As a facilitator, you have to be flexible and ready to respond to new information you learn from the group.

THE ROLE OF THE FACILITATOR

Every human being has the capacity to imagine and create. Our job as facilitators is to liberate the expression of this imagination and creativity. At the beginning of a workshop or series of workshops, many things have not yet been defined by the participants, such as how they relate together as a group and, perhaps, the themes they will deal with. This is an exciting moment, as the lack of definition opens up endless possibilities.

Participants need to be able to generate and explore content for themselves, taking risks and experimenting and rehearsing for real life. We can facilitate this by providing structure and form for the workshops. To create a safe space where risks can be taken, we need to consider physical and emotional safety, trust, integration between group members and the rules by which the group operates. This section raises important issues we need to consider when facilitating any workshop, not just those employing theatre-based techniques.

SAFETY

All participants in a workshop need to feel secure, both physically and emotionally (this includes the facilitator). The facilitator can achieve this in part by defining some boundaries with the group: the overall aim of the sessions, limits and rules of behaviour. These boundaries give a general structure to the work. Within this structure, the group can feel safe, they are conscious of the limits and know that the other participants are as well, but are free to create within them. And the safer we feel, the more prepared we will be to run risks. That is why both the facilitator and the group have to stick to the rules that have been established, even if this creates the possibility of conflict. The group might decide for example, not to let anyone join the workshop if they are more than 15 minutes late as this would disrupt the workshop process. The question then arises, how would the group deal with this in practice? This, and any other dilemmas that may arise, need to be discussed when the rules are set. Rules should include a confidentiality contract to ensure that what is said in the group stays within the group.

See the section **Beginnings** in the manual for suggestions of exercises you can use for setting rules in a group.

PHYSICAL SAFETY

In any group, different participants will have different strengths and weaknesses. Physical strength is no exception. When you are planning a workshop, you should take into account:

- The physical strength of all the participants.
- Are there some people who simply won't be able to participate as fully as others?
- Are you planning for the whole group?
- What physical limitations do individuals have?

You should plan your workshop based on the physical possibilities of the participants as individuals and as a group. Occasionally, a whole group may share a physical characteristic which defines the type of exercises you can do. For example, in a series of workshops with textile workers in Lima, Peru, I used a series of exercises based on hearing and rhythm and realised that the group was having difficulties. Eventually I stopped the session and asked the participants why this was. I discovered that they worked with heavy machinery all day, without adequate protective headgear and that most of them had hearing problems.

Workshops often require participants to use their bodies in unfamiliar ways. Introduce different types of movement work gradually to give participants a chance to accustom their bodies to new challenges. Be aware of the danger of injuries caused by 'too much too soon' such as muscle strains and avoid excluding participants who do not feel physically able to keep up with others. You may want to give participants the choice to opt out of exercises, although this can be used by some as an excuse to sit and watch the rest of the group. If someone doesn't want to participate think carefully about why this is. They may need special attention or they may not be physically able to do the exercise.

CULTURAL SENSITIVITY

- Be sensitive to cultural codes which may govern behaviours in individual communities or work spaces.

- Participants may not be accustomed to physical contact between men and women, and even asking the group to hold hands in a circle may prove a problem.

- Local dress may also restrict movement and therefore the type of exercises you can incorporate into your work.

FACILITATOR OR PARTICIPANT?

As the main guardian of group safety, the facilitator has to be able to step back from the group and monitor progress and problems. It is very difficult to do this whilst participating in an exercise, so your role is often that of participant observer. This is especially true when you ask participants to close their eyes; you should never close your eyes at the same time as there must always be someone who has the trust of the group present to monitor what is happening.

By inviting participants to explore the possibility for change in their lives, you are inviting them to take risks and are therefore responsible for their emotional safety. Challenge the group emotionally, but always ensure that participants know there is a safety net to catch them. Experimentation does involve risk but should not be deadly.

Although workshops often focus on life skills or the resolution of conflicts from participants' own lives, they should still be clearly separate spaces from the rest of the participants' lives. Warm ups mark the beginning of a session and help participants to focus. Closing exercises mark the end of a session and prepare the group for the transition back to their lives outside the group. Another way of marking this difference is to always use fictitious names for characters in improvisations rather than the names of group members.

INTEGRATION

A new group often comes together for some stated common purpose, but each group member arrives with their own agenda, their own skills and experience and a need to establish their identity within the group. Working as a group means negotiating compromise as individuals find common ground, shared objectives and a way of working together. The facilitator's job is to establish collaboration, co-operation, equality of opportunity and respect within the group. Once these are in place, the group will be able to take risks and develop new ideas.

SETTING THE RULES

Explain the rules of each exercise carefully, but be careful not to give too much information to the group at once. Instead, you can build up more complicated exercises stage by stage. It is often useful to demonstrate an exercise using volunteers from the group before you start to play.

If there is a misunderstanding about the rules of an exercise, or an exercise simply fails, participants can become frustrated and start to blame one another. If this happens, restart the exercise or think about ways of restructuring it with the group. Groups have come up with many interesting variations on games in this way.

ADVICE FROM OTHER FACILITATORS IN BRAZIL

These comments were generated from one of the exercises from the manual: **Ex. 126 Letter to an Alien**, carried out in training sessions in Brazil and Peru during research for this book:

*You have to take into account **observation**, be **organised** and **objective**, without forgetting to be original. The person **orienting** the group should **listen** attentively and be **opportune** in their interventions.*

*The facilitator should not be anxious or omnipotent. It is fundamental to be quite **objective**, without forgetting to be **optimistic** and a good **listener** to the needs of the group.*

*Above all, you should be **responsible**. Be **realistic** about all the activities you decide to do … and realise all your ideas and projects. Meanwhile, you have to be **reasonable** and have **respect** for other people. You have to be a bit of a **rocker** to **realise** all your work successfully and always be **receptive** to new ideas.*

ADVICE FROM OTHER FACILITATORS IN PERU

*The first thing you have to be is **loyal** to yourself and you must respect the **liberty** that others have to speak. It will help you if you are really **eloquent**. Show your skills as a **leader** and don't forget to always let dialogue flow with **liberty**.*

*First, you should have the spirit of a **renovator**, coupled with **respect** and **responsibility**, don't forget to always be **rapid** and to take **risks**.*

*A facilitator contributes to the **transformation** of various situations. To this end, you will use **therapeutic techniques** as well as others, all with **tolerance** and a respect for different cultures. What is more, watch the **time**, you need to be daring and know your own **temperament** so that you don't fall into **torpor**!*

SECTION 1

BEGINNINGS
WARM UPS, BUILDING GROUP, WORKING TOGETHER, FOCUS AND CONCENTRATION

1	KITES AND BALLOONS
OBJECTIVES	Identify hopes and fears
FOCUS	Low
ENERGY	Low
NUMBERS	3+
DURATION	20 to 30 min
MATERIAL	Sheets of paper cut into balloon and kite shapes
	Coloured pens or pencils
	Large sheets of paper
	Marker pen
STAGES	In groups of 3 to 5, participants discuss their fears and expectations in relation to the workshop, listing their fears on the balloons (so they can be exploded) and their expectations on the kites (so that they can rise). The groups do not have to write their names on their work.
	The groups put their balloons and kites into a pile in the middle of the room and take another kite and balloon from the pile.
	Each group now reads out these fears and expectations to everyone.
	The facilitator summarises all the fears and expectations on a large sheet of paper.

FROM THE FIELD

Discussing our fears and expectations like this was great because we were able to get a general view of these themes from the group and this helped us to create a contract of work which took account of the whole group.

It was an interesting way to find out the expectations of the group. I noticed that in general, the participants had difficulty expressing what they really wanted. It was difficult for us to transfer what we had written on the kites and balloons to a larger summary for the whole group, because we didn't really understand what the others were trying to say.

2	GALLERY OF HOPES AND FEARS
OBJECTIVES	Identify hopes and fears
	Issue-based work
FOCUS	Low
ENERGY	Medium
NUMBERS	4+
DURATION	20 to 30 min
MATERIAL	None

STAGES	Ask the group to divide into pairs: **A** (the sculptors) and **B** (modelling clay). Remind the group to work in silence.
	Explain that in each pair, **A** has 2 minutes to model **B** into a sculpture (a frozen image) of a fear they have regarding the work they are about to start in the group.
	After 2 minutes, ask all the sculptors to move away from their works, which should now be displayed in the centre of the room as a gallery.
	Ask the sculptors to group similar sculptures together.
	Ask the group to look at each group of images and suggest words to describe what they can see.
	The facilitator should note these ideas on a large sheet of paper for the group to see.
	Now, the original pairs swap roles: **B** models **A**, creating an image of their hopes and the reading process is repeated.
	Finally, ask the group to look at the summary of all their fears and expectations and to add any that have not been included.
	This summary can now be used to write a contract of work with the group and to anticipate and talk through problems they might face.

HINTS

If you are working with a small number of people, ask both **A** and **B** to model fears and hopes. This will give you more material to work with.

You could also use this exercise for issue-based work.

FROM THE FIELD

I used this exercise to evaluate teamwork in my institution and to discuss the educative process.

3	THE CONTRACT
OBJECTIVES	Establish rules for the group
FOCUS	Low
ENERGY	Low
NUMBERS	4+
DURATION	20 min
MATERIAL	Sheets of paper
	Coloured pens
	Large sheets of paper
	Marker pens
STAGES	Write each fear and expectation generated by the group on separate sheets of paper, place them in 2 columns (one of fears, one of expectations) on the floor. Between them place a large sheet of blank paper.
	Ask the group to re-order the columns, matching up corresponding fears and expectations where they can.
	The group now thinks of rules which they will all agree to follow to help meet these expectations and dispel the fears.
	Write these rules on the blank piece of paper and either pin it on the wall or distribute a copy to each group member.

HINTS

You can use the fears and expectations generated in **Ex. 1 Kites and Balloons** for this exercise.

4	MY NAME IN ACTION
OBJECTIVES	Warm up
	Breaking the ice
	Building group identity
FOCUS	Low
ENERGY	Medium
NUMBERS	3+
DURATION	10 min
MATERIAL	None
STAGES	Ask the group to form a circle.

Each participant thinks of a word which starts with the first sound of their name, and has something to do with their personality (for example, Energetic Emma). Each word should be accompanied by a gesture to illustrate it.

A participant goes to the centre of the circle, says their name, the word and completes their gesture.

The rest of the group takes 2 steps towards the centre of the circle and repeats the name, word and gesture twice.

The next person in the circle then shows their name, word and gesture for the group to repeat.

EXTENSION

After everyone has presented themselves, indicate a person and ask the group to remember their name, word or gesture. Most people will be able to remember at least 1 of the 3 for each person.

HINTS

This technique allows us to reveal ourselves to a group on a first meeting and helps the group to see each other beyond references of social class or status.

The exercise can help us to perceive levels of self-esteem in the participants.

FROM THE FIELD

This technique helped me to get to know the group who I was going to start work with.

I used this technique in a children's home with girls, and one of them, who was always very afraid of participating, was very quiet, amazed everyone when she went into the middle of the circle and said 'Silvia – salta' [Jumping Silvia] – and jumped into the air. After the session, she came up and said: "it's not so difficult to speak. We shouldn't be frightened of what we want to do!"

I used this game with a group of teachers who seemed quite resistant to the idea of the workshop. The exercise relaxed the group, people seemed less resistant and we were able to get on with the work, which I thought might be impossible.

It was difficult to get the children to loosen up at first, we had to encourage and motivate them, some of them preferred to remain silent, which we had to respect.

I used this with children with learning difficulties. They associated sounds to their names rather than words. The exercise revealed abilities that the children have which we hadn't perceived before through other activities. I am going to include these exercises in assessments we carry out with the children.

This is a good ice-breaker for people who don't know each other yet. It is very creative and brings together sounds and images which help the participants learn each other's names. When I used this technique, I asked myself how much information it could reveal about the participants. Even though this isn't the objective of the exercise, it ends up projecting the subjective imaginations of the individual. For example, when I did the exercise with adolescents who live in urban areas, many of them are linked to the Hip Hop culture and the words they associated with their names were very linked to urban life, Break Dance, Rap, graffiti and the violence that they co-exist with every day. In the case of adolescents and children from rural areas, the words and gestures which they linked to their names, were associated with catholic saints, fruits, plants, work tools such as scythes and spades.

5	MARIA, MARIA, MARIA
OBJECTIVES	Warm up
	Breaking the ice
	Focus and concentration
FOCUS	High / Low
ENERGY	Medium
NUMBERS	4+
DURATION	10 min
MATERIAL	None
STAGES	Ask the group to form a circle.
	Ask a volunteer to stand in the centre of the circle and to say the name of another group member 3 times, very quickly. For example, 'Maria, Maria, Maria!'
	The person who has been called has to answer with their own name before the person in the centre has called them for the third time.
	If the person called manages to answer in time, the same person stays in the centre and tries again with another name. If they do not manage to say their own name in time, they swap places with the person in the middle.

HINTS
As the exercise progresses it gets increasingly difficult to get out of the centre as levels of concentration increase.

6	NAME TAG
OBJECTIVES	Warm up
	Breaking the ice
	Building group identity
	Generate energy
FOCUS	Low
ENERGY	High
NUMBERS	4+
DURATION	10 min
MATERIAL	None

STAGES	This is a game of tag where there is no running, only fast walking.
	Ask a volunteer to be 'on'. They must walk around the room with 1 arm outstretched with the palm of their hand facing forward. Their objective is to *'tag'* someone with this hand.
	The group walks slowly round the room avoiding being tagged.
	To save yourself from being tagged, you can say the name of another participant. If you do this before you are touched, that person is now automatically 'on' and you are safe.
	However, if you get tagged before you say a name, then you are now 'on'.
	Each participant has 3 lives. So once they have been tagged 3 times, they must first tag someone else and then leave the game.

HINTS

If you are playing with a lot of people, each participant should have only 2 lives.
The rules sound quite complicated, so the best way to explain them is to do a demonstration with 4 or 5 people.
This game is very good for breaking down barriers and releasing all the natural tension found at the beginning of a new project or group.
After this technique, the group could try **Ex. 63 Image Tag**.

FROM THE FIELD

I've played this game with 3 people and 30.

This is a good game to play with older people as it is a version of tag without any running.

I used this game with a group that wanted to set up a gay movement in their city. We adapted it so that every time someone was tagged, the game froze for a second while that person explained why they had gone to the workshop.

7	SHAKING HANDS
OBJECTIVES	Warm up
	Breaking the ice
	Working together
	Closing a workshop
FOCUS	Low
ENERGY	Medium
NUMBERS	5+
DURATION	5 min
MATERIAL	None
STAGES	Explain that the aim of the game is to shake hands with everyone in the room.
	Ask each participant to shake someone's hand and freeze in this position. With their free hand they should shake the hand of someone else.
	They then release the hand of the first hand they shook.
	Participants move around the room, but must always be shaking hands with at least one person.
	The game continues until everyone has shaken hands with everyone else.

8	HOW MANY WAYS TO SAY HELLO?
SOURCE	Boal, Augusto (1992)
OBJECTIVES	Warm up
	Working together
	Building group identity
FOCUS	Medium
ENERGY	Medium
NUMBERS	3+
DURATION	15 min
MATERIAL	None
STAGES	The group stands in a circle.
	Explain that they are going to find out how many ways they know to say 'hello'.
	One volunteer takes 2 steps into the middle of the circle and says 'hello'
	accompanied by a gesture (such as a wave).
	The rest of the group take 2 steps into the middle and repeat the word and gesture
	twice, then move back.
	Other participants enter one by one with new ways of saying hello.

EXTENSION

Use different words related to an issue you are working on.

Use animal sounds instead of words.

In bilingual communities, explore all the different words and gestures used for greetings.

FROM THE FIELD

There are words in bilingual communities in the Amazon rainforest that express values or feelings about a name, for example, there is a name that means 'strong heart'. So you can use and highlight the richness of each native language in this game.

I used this game in a workshop in Peru, with people who didn't know each other at all. They came from varied backgrounds: indigenous rural workers, NGO workers from the city, Afro Peruvians and people from other countries. Through the game we discovered a richness of expression in the group which surprised us all. It was a moment of true cultural exchange, which bonded us for the days to come.

9	THINGS IN COMMON
OBJECTIVES	Warm up
	Breaking the ice
	Building group identity
FOCUS	Low
ENERGY	Low
NUMBERS	3+
DURATION	10 min
MATERIAL	None
STAGES	Ask the participants to form groups of 3, preferably with people they don't know.
	Explain that each group has 5 minutes to discover 3 things that the 3 people have in
	common which each other.
	Highlight that the 3 things in common cannot be too obvious, for example,
	nationality, hair colour etc.

13

Call everyone into a circle and ask each group to present the things they have in common to the whole group.

FROM THE FIELD

There are always interesting things to learn about people even if you think you know them well.

I used this technique to examine the identity of the group and it produced a rich discussion.

I like this technique because it's really easy to do, easy for the group to understand and produces a quick answer from the group.

This technique stimulated intimacy between the participants. Even though they had known each other for some time, they found out new things about each other.

10	THREE LIES
OBJECTIVES	Warm up
	Breaking the ice
FOCUS	High
ENERGY	Low
NUMBERS	2+
DURATION	10 min
MATERIAL	None
STAGES	Participants sit in a circle.
	Ask everyone to tell the group 3 facts about themselves. Two should be true and 1 a lie.
	The group has to guess which is the false fact.

HINTS

If the group is large, play this game in small groups.

11	WHAT DO WE SHARE?
OBJECTIVES	Warm up
	Breaking the ice
	Building group identity
FOCUS	Low
ENERGY	Medium
NUMBERS	8+
DURATION	10 min
MATERIAL	None
STAGES	Ask participants to walk around the room filling up all the space.
	Explain that you are going to shout out a question (see suggestions below).
	When participants hear the question (for example, what's your favourite food?) they move around the room, repeating their answer as they go.
	When participants meet people with the same answer they team up with them and continue walking.

Repeat the activity with other questions.

Ask participants to shout out questions for the group to answer.

Suggested questions:

Favourite food?

Your job?

Number of people in your family?

Number of children?

Favourite TV programme?

12	WHO ARE WE?
OBJECTIVES	Warm up
	Breaking the ice
	Building group identity
FOCUS	Low
ENERGY	Low
NUMBERS	4+
DURATION	10 min
MATERIAL	None
STAGES	Explain to the group that they are going to respond to the question 'who are we?' Each person in turn should answer this question with a sentence, for example 'we work for NGOs', 'we are young', 'we are parents'. After each response, the participants raise their hands if they feel they are included in that particular description.

HINTS

This technique can be the starting point for a discussion or piece of practical work about the group identity. For example, 'is the group as homogenous as we thought?'

FROM THE FIELD

This is an effective exercise for stimulating self-reflection and a process of bridge building between participants. It works on self-esteem without mentioning the word!

13	SELF-PORTRAIT
OBJECTIVES	Warm up
	Breaking the ice
	Building group identity
FOCUS	High
ENERGY	Low
NUMBERS	4+
DURATION	20 min
MATERIAL	A4 paper
	Colour pens and pencils
	Masking tape

Ask each participant to draw their self-portrait and to write underneath 3 moments in their lives that have in some way led them to participate in today's workshop.
Remind the group not to sign their self-portraits but to keep them anonymous.
Collect all the portraits and hang them on the walls.
Invite the group to walk around and try to identify each group member from their portrait.

HINTS

This technique can be used to evaluate a project or to close a series of workshops, by asking participants to write 3 moments that were important to them during the process.

FROM THE FIELD

Instead of moments in their lives, we asked participants to describe 3 things they normally do at home, for example: eating, getting dressed and cleaning.

14	FRUIT SALAD
OBJECTIVES	Warm up
	Breaking the ice
	Building group identity
	Uncover underlying issues
FOCUS	Low
ENERGY	High
NUMBERS	4+
DURATION	15 min
MATERIAL	Chairs
STAGES	**FIRST STAGE**

FIRST STAGE

The group sits on chairs in a circle.
A volunteer removes their chair and stands in the middle of the circle.
Go around the circle naming each person 1 of 3 fruits (e.g. apple, pear, banana).
The person in the middle calls one of the fruits, for example '**apples**'. All the apples then have to change chairs, while the caller tries to sit down.
If the caller shouts 'FRUIT SALAD' everyone has to change places.

SECOND STAGE

The rules are basically the same, but instead of fruits, the caller says: CHANGE PLACES IF… you like chocolate, you have children, you live with your parents, you have shouted at someone today…
The group generally starts by using things they can see such as clothes or hair colour. Explain that this game is a good way of finding things out about each other, such as where people live, who they live with, what they like and don't like.

VARIATION

Limit questions to a certain issue you are working on with the group. This is a good way to research and exchange related personal experiences.

HINTS

If you do not have any chairs, you can use circles drawn on the floor.

The level of intimacy varies from group to group. I have seen a group of people who don't know each other very well keeping the questions related to very superficial things. But I've also played with a group of adult factory workers who knew each other very well. They started with questions around their likes and dislikes, but eventually moved on to questions about their emotions, depression and domestic violence. This makes the game sound intrusive. But the participants generally respect each other's limits.

In this exercise, you can ask whatever you want to, but you can also choose whether to answer a question or not. If you don't want to answer, then you just don't get up and change places.

With a group of young men working on issues of violence, we used this exercise to discuss what acts they considered to be violent or not. It generated a lot of discussion.

Because this exercise is done in a circle and uses physical movement, it brings questions alive and mobilises participants, so the danger of a discussion becoming monotonous is reduced. Generally, the participants act as moderators, encouraging questions and setting clear limits between what is an exercise and what is therapy. The tendency is for the questions to dig quite deep and they can go in a therapeutic direction which isn't really appropriate for this game. When the facilitator says for example, 'change places if you like art', the people who identify with this question make eye contact, share and exchange experiences and tastes.

15	RECOGNISING HANDS
OBJECTIVES	Warm up
	Breaking the ice
	Focus and concentration
	Building group identity
	Working together
FOCUS	Low
ENERGY	Low
NUMBERS	6+
DURATION	10 min
MATERIAL	None
STAGES	The group forms pairs.
	Ask each pair to examine each other's hands so that they could recognise them by touch. Whilst doing this, participants can explain details related to their hands – stories related to rings, scars etc.
	After 5 minutes, the pairs separate and everyone begins to walk around the room with their eyes closed.
	Tell the participants that they should find their partner by identifying their hands.

FROM THE FIELD

The participants didn't worry about their differences but only about finding their partner. It exercised their senses, especially touch, which is so important for older people who may be losing their sight or hearing.

This is a good exercise to use before work that requires people to touch each other, because it uses parts of the body that we don't mind touching or being touched.

16	THE MAD CHICKEN
OBJECTIVES	Warm up
	Generate energy
	Closing a workshop
FOCUS	Low
ENERGY	High
NUMBERS	2+
DURATION	5 min
MATERIAL	None
STAGES	Explain that the whole group is going to count from 1 to 8 whilst shaking their right hands in the air. Repeat whilst shaking left hands.
	The group then count to 8 whilst shaking first the right leg and then the left.
	The group repeats these 4 actions, but this time they only count up to 4.
	Repeat again, counting to 2.
	Finally count only to 1, repeating this last part twice.

VARIATION

You can also use a count from 1 to 8, increasing the number of times each limb is shaken out. This stimulates rapidity and rhythm in the group as the numbers rise.

HINTS

This is a good exercise to do after a break or lunch because it raises the energy of the group and it is quick and easy.

FROM THE FIELD

I love this, because it raises the spirits of people, they leave behind their worries for a moment.

I used this with women in a rural area. They are often very reserved, but you could see that they were very happy, so much so that they changed the name of the exercise to 'Galinha Turuleca', which means mad chicken in the Quechua language. When they were feeling tired, they would ask me for this exercise!

With girls in an orphanage who had to get up at 5am, this was marvellous. After doing the exercise, they felt full of motivation to start their activities for the day.

This helped the girls I work with to count. It helped them to lose the fear of participating in activities and filled them with energy.

17	TOUCH 3 THINGS
OBJECTIVES	Warm up
	Generate energy
FOCUS	Low
ENERGY	High
NUMBERS	3+
DURATION	5 min
MATERIAL	None
STAGES	Ask the group to walk around the room using all the space.
	Explain that you are going to say a list of things that the group has to touch as quickly as possible. For example: 3 legs, 2 walls, and 5 feet.

FROM THE FIELD

I used this with a group that needed to build some trust with each other, so the last thing I asked them to touch was the hands of the other participants.

This game was important for us in our workshop because we work with peasant farmers whose reflexes are generally slow and this works on the speed of their reactions.

We used this exercise whenever the group was feeling sleepy and distracted.

18	THE KNEE GAME
OBJECTIVES	Warm up Generate energy
FOCUS	Low
ENERGY	High
NUMBERS	2+
DURATION	5 min
MATERIAL	None
STAGES	Ask the group to form pairs and find a space in the room to work. Explain that the objective of the game is to win points by touching the knees of their partners whilst protecting their own knees from being touched. The winner in each pair is the one who scores 3 points first.

FROM THE FIELD

This is a really good warm up. I used it with young people who were really fired up to continue working in the group afterwards. It was cold outside, but we didn't feel it anymore.

I think that with adolescents and children it is better to ask them to touch their partner's knees with only 2 fingers, to avoid hard slaps and any bruises.

19	COLLECTING COINS
OBJECTIVES	Warm up Generate energy
FOCUS	Low
ENERGY	High
NUMBERS	3+
DURATION	5 min
MATERIAL	A coin for each participant
STAGES	Ask participants to put a coin on the flat of their hands and to put their hands behind their back. Explain that they cannot close their hands at any point during the game. The objective is to collect as many coins as possible by taking them from other players and placing them in the hands behind their backs. While they are trying to collect coins, they also have to try and stop other players from taking theirs. The winners are the players who collect the most coins.

VARIATION

Give a piece of material or a scarf to each player and ask them to tuck this into the back of their trousers, skirt or belt. Each player has to collect as many pieces of cloth as possible without losing their own.
You can also play the game in pairs.

20	SNAKE IN THE GRASS
OBJECTIVES	Warm up
	Generate energy
FOCUS	Medium
ENERGY	Medium
NUMBERS	5+
DURATION	10 min
MATERIAL	Masking tape
STAGES	Mark a square on the floor with masking tape – the size depends on the number of people playing, but should be big enough for the group to move around in.
	Ask a volunteer to be the snake. She will try to catch the other players.
	The snake lies on the floor inside the square and the other players stand around her touching her with just 1 finger.
	When the facilitator shouts 'SNAKE,' the snake rises up onto all fours.
	The objective is for the snake to catch players and for the players to avoid being caught without stepping outside the marked square.
	When the snake catches someone they are 'out' and stand around the outside of the square watching to see if any of the remaining players step outside the square.
	The game continues until there is only 1 player left inside the square with the snake.

FROM THE FIELD

We used this game differently, with the snake walking slowly around the outside of the square. We reduced the size of the square as the serpent caught people.

This worked really well with a group of adults and a group of older people that already knew each other. The players laughed a lot and got really involved in the game.

21	RUNNING THROUGH MUD
OBJECTIVES	Warm up
	Generate energy
FOCUS	Low
ENERGY	High
NUMBERS	4+
DURATION	15 min
MATERIAL	Music
STAGES	Ask the group to walk around the room using up all the space and moving with the music.
	Give instructions for the group to follow. For example:

Run quickly	Walk using the outside of your feet
Walk slowly	Walk as if you were treading on cotton wool, mud, ice ...
Hop on one leg	

22	MUSICAL CHAIRS
OBJECTIVES	Warm up
	Generate energy
FOCUS	Low
ENERGY	High
NUMBERS	6+
DURATION	10 min
MATERIAL	Chairs
	Music
STAGES	Ask the participants to take a chair each and put the chairs in a circle with the seats facing outwards.
	Remove one of the chairs so that there is one more participant than chairs.
	Ask the group to walk around the outside of the circle to the sound of the music.
	When the music stops, the players should try to sit down on one of the chairs.
	The player who does not find a seat is out of the game and one more chair is removed.
	The game continues until there is 1 player left.

FROM THE FIELD

I used this technique to observe and reflect on the capacity for negotiation and inclusion in the group. How much competition and pushing is permissible in a group activity? Is it an individual game or can you co-operate with other players? It produced a really interesting discussion.

Children in rural Amazon communities really enjoyed this. But I had to be careful that they didn't hurt themselves or start competing too much between each other.

23	THE CIRCLE AND THE CROSS
SOURCE	Boal, Augusto (1992)
OBJECTIVES	Warm up
	Focus and concentration
FOCUS	Low
ENERGY	Low
NUMBERS	2+
DURATION	5 min
MATERIAL	None
STAGES	Ask the group to form a circle.
	Tell the participants to draw a circle in the air with their right hands.
	Then ask them to draw a cross in the air with their left arms.
	Now ask the group to try to do both actions at the same time.

VARIATION:

Ask the participants to draw a circle with their left feet.

Then, ask them to write their names in the air with their right hands.

Finally, ask the group to draw the circle and their names at the same time.

24	MASSAGE
OBJECTIVES	Warm up
	Generate energy
	Working together
	Closing a workshop
FOCUS	Low
ENERGY	Medium
NUMBERS	4+
DURATION	5 min
MATERIAL	None
STAGES	The participants walk around the room.
	The facilitator shouts a part of the body, for example, arm, back or foot.
	Participants find someone in the room and start massaging that part of their body whilst repeating its name, for example, 'arm, arm, arm'.
	Remind participants that they cannot massage the person who is massaging them.
	This will create various massage chains in the room.
	Repeat with various parts of the body.

25	EARTHQUAKE
OBJECTIVES	Warm up
	Working together
	Generate energy
	Issue: family
	Closing a workshop
FOCUS	Low
ENERGY	High
NUMBERS	6+
DURATION	10 min
MATERIAL	None
STAGES	Form groups of 3, and ask a volunteer to stand in the middle of the room – they are the caller.
	Ask 2 people from each trio to stand facing each other and touch hands above their heads, making the roof and walls of the house.
	The third person stands between the other 2 (between the walls) – they are the people.
	Ask the caller to stand in the middle of the room. Explain that they can call one of 3 commands: if they call 'WALLS', the 2 walls separate and form another house around an inhabitant. The people do not move.
	If the caller shouts 'PEOPLE', the people run inside another house. The walls do not move.
	If the caller shouts 'EARTHQUAKE', everyone changes places. They can also change from being a wall to being a person or vice versa.
	Meanwhile, the caller has to fit into one of the groups as a wall or an inhabitant, leaving a new person in the middle as the caller.

FROM THE FIELD

This game is really popular with adolescents. But it was also really popular with a group of prison directors.

I used this with deaf children in an orphanage. It worked really well with the 2 groups and they asked to do it again and again.

I used this game to work on the themes of housing and citizenship with a group of young men. After playing, the group began to talk about where they lived, how they lived, what their relationship was with their neighbourhood and their houses.

I used the game to generate a discussion about family. The participants spoke about the diverse family models they had and how it was to live in their families, how work was shared, family income etc.

The adolescent and young adult men managed to integrate quickly, because the idea of not losing became more important than inter-group differences or fear of the unknown.

In the Peruvian jungle, there aren't any earthquakes; you could use another natural phenomenon like a flood or a hurricane.

26	THE SHRINKING NEWSPAPER
OBJECTIVES	Warm up
	Breaking the ice
	Working together
FOCUS	Low
ENERGY	Medium
NUMBERS	6+
DURATION	10 min
MATERIAL	Newspaper
	Masking tape
STAGES	Place a square of newspaper on the floor (various sheets taped together), big enough for the group to stand on.
	Explain that the participants cannot touch the floor, walls or furniture but they can touch the newspaper (the whole group will probably stand on the newspaper).
	Ask everyone to step off the newspaper while you reduce it in size. Then repeat the exercise.
	Carry on until you cannot reduce the size of the paper any further.
	Encourage the participants to find other ways to reach their objective (sitting on each other for example).

HINTS

Instead of newspaper you can use a square of masking tape.

Give participants half a piece of newspaper and ask them to dance on it without stepping off the paper. Then fold the paper in half and ask them to keep dancing. Continue until the paper is about the size of their feet. This stimulates them into using other parts of their bodies, not just their feet.

27	BEAR OF POITIERS
SOURCE	Boal, Augusto (1992)
OBJECTIVES	Warm up
	Focus and concentration
FOCUS	Low
ENERGY	Low
NUMBERS	8+
DURATION	15 min
MATERIAL	None
STAGES	Ask 3 volunteers to be the bears. The rest of the group are woodcutters.
	Ask the bears to leave the room. Tell them to enter when they hear 'HERE COME THE BEARS'.
	Meanwhile, construct a scene with the woodcutters cutting down trees, singing...
	Explain that there is a problem. There are lots of bears in the area. They are very hungry and they eat people! But, luckily, they don't like to eat other things, so the only way to stay safe when the bears arrive is to convince the bears that you are an object – like a tree or a stone.
	Explain to the woodcutters that when they hear 'HERE COME THE BEARS' they should run and find a place to freeze.
	Shout 'HERE COME THE BEARS'.
	When the bears come in they find food by trying to make the woodcutters move.
	If a woodcutter moves they become a bear.
	The game continues until there is only 1 woodcutter left.

28	CAREFUL, HERE COMES THE SHARK!
OBJECTIVES	Warm up
	Building group identity
	Working together
FOCUS	Low
ENERGY	High
NUMBERS	4+
DURATION	10 min
MATERIAL	Masking tape
STAGES	Mark a square on the floor with masking tape and explain that this is a lifeboat. The group has been shipwrecked in shark-infested water.
	Tell the participants to get into the lifeboat and explain that there is only enough drinking water for 1 person. The objective is to stay in the boat.
	Anyone who falls out of the boat, or puts an arm or leg outside of it is eaten by the sharks and is out of the game.
	The group generally pushes each other until only 1 person is left.

	HINTS
	This is a game of strategy not physical force. You can opt to remind the group of this before they play.
	This is a good game for working on co-operation and conflict resolution.

FROM THE FIELD

Doing this game as a warm up, various groups raised the point of why only 1 person survives. This is an interesting question to raise in a workshop on co-operation and constructing the identity of the group.

This game awoke the need in the participants to think and rethink the group, and why suddenly if you want to survive you have to throw other people overboard... After the game comes the reflection ... how is our group going? How do we fit together as individuals, the game highlighted all these points and was very useful.

*This game can be very challenging with adolescents...
I think it's dangerous because adolescents have so much energy, which can be difficult to cope with, and if there is any animosity in the group this type of exercise can be a bit complicated to do.*

This was a quite stressful exercise. It is difficult to do something that is different from what we have learnt to do our whole lives. It is difficult to dominate the animal instinct that exists within us, that instinct of self-preservation.

This exercise deals with the dispute and marking of territory between people. The shark is a metaphor for our daily lives, the fight for professional recognition, how people protect their own interests. The marked space – the life boat, where everyone is together and trying to keep away from the sharks whilst at the same time throwing other people to them – represents the social space where we interact and dispute with others: university, family, study groups, work places and personal relationships with partners.

With young people from an urban area, instead of throwing each other out of the boat immediately, these people spent a long time holding onto each other, showing a great spirit of mutual support. There was no suggestion on the part of the facilitator to do this, it was completely spontaneous.

29	STRANGE POSITIONS
SOURCE	Boal, Augusto (1992)
OBJECTIVES	Warm up Working together
FOCUS	Low
ENERGY	Medium
NUMBERS	2+
DURATION	15 min
MATERIAL	None
STAGES	Ask the group to form pairs. Give instructions which the participants follow without speaking. For example: 'Touch the shoulder of your partner with your thumb. Now, without moving your thumb, touch your partner's shoulder with your nose. Now touch your partner's knee with your heel.' Each new instruction builds on the previous one – the facilitator continues giving instructions until no more can be added. Restart the exercise with groups of 3, then 4, then 5 until the whole group is working together.

I noted that the group really tried to work together to achieve the objective, and beat the limits of their own bodies.

This exercise stimulates confidence in your partner because you count on him to make the movements.

I'd only use this with a group of people who already know each other quite well, because of the physical intimacy involved.

We had been working with a group and having problems trying to get them to move and to think about the issue of personal space. We were very worried about this, but we decided to relax and to try some games. We let the game continue and watched how they subverted each other's actions and were quite cheeky with each other.

30	SEA AND SHORE
OBJECTIVES	Warm up Focus and concentration
FOCUS	Medium
ENERGY	High
NUMBERS	6+
DURATION	5 min
MATERIAL	Chalk or tape
STAGES	Divide the space (with chalk or tape) into 2 halves; one of them is the sea and the other the shore. Ask the group to start the game by standing in one of the spaces. Explain that, when the facilitator shouts 'SEA' they should all jump or run to the sea, when the facilitator shouts 'SHORE' they should go to the other side. People who jump to the wrong side leave the game until there is only 1 person left. **VARIATION** Instead of using 'SEA' and 'SHORE' you can use colours, place names or words related to a particular theme.

31	WRITING WITH THE BODY
OBJECTIVES	Warm up Working together
FOCUS	Low
ENERGY	Medium
NUMBERS	4+
DURATION	20 min
MATERIAL	None
STAGES	Ask the participants to make groups of 4 to 8 (depending on the overall number of participants). Explain that each group is going to draw letters, numbers or whole words with their bodies. Tell the group they have 2 minutes to complete the task.

The facilitator should start with simple numbers or letters (T, F, 7) and progress to more complicated ones (A, Z, 24).

You can also ask the group to form whole words.

Join up various groups until everyone is working together.

VARIATION

Ask the group to draw objects, for example, a boat, a house or a tree.

32	ROMEO AND JULIET
OBJECTIVES	Warm up
	Working together
FOCUS	Low
ENERGY	Medium
NUMBERS	6+
DURATION	5 min
MATERIAL	None
STAGES	Ask 1 volunteer to play Romeo and another to play Juliet.

The objective of the game is for Romeo to catch Juliet.

Everyone except Romeo walks around the room.

With his eyes closed, Romeo has to find Juliet by calling her name and listening out for her answer.

If Romeo calls Juliet, only she can answer (by calling Romeo). But the rest of the group can try to confuse Romeo by calling out his name at any time.

The game finishes when Romeo catches Juliet.

VARIATION

Two Romeos try to find their 'Juliets' at the same time.

33	KNOTS
OBJECTIVES	Working together
	Non-verbal communication
FOCUS	Low / High
ENERGY	Medium
NUMBERS	10+
DURATION	15 min
MATERIAL	None
STAGES	Ask 2 volunteers to leave the room.

The rest of the group holds hands in a circle.

Without letting go of each others' hands, the group twists themselves into a knot.

Call the volunteers into the room and give them 3 minutes to undo the knot. Tell them that they cannot touch anyone, or make any gestures, they can only give instructions verbally, for example, turn around to your left, step over that leg etc.

The facilitator times how long it takes to complete the task.

The process is repeated with new volunteers. This time, the volunteers cannot speak, but have to undo the knot using their hands to guide the group.

Finally, ask the whole group to make a new knot and to undo it themselves. They will achieve this very quickly.

If you are using this exercise in a training workshop, the following discussion may be useful:

DISCUSSION

What does this game tell us about verbal and non-verbal language? Which instructions were the clearest?

What does that tell us about giving instructions?

Which was the quickest way to untie the knot? (This is usually the group untying itself).

Can you relate this to your work or the organisation you work for?

FROM THE FIELD

This exercise works on notions of communication and the problems related to group work.

This made me remember the many times people have come from outside to facilitate something, to untie knots, but many times these facilitators just complicated things.

When you orientate someone verbally it can get complicated. Touch or other forms of non-verbal communication can really help.

34	POINTS OF CONTACT
OBJECTIVES	Warm up
	Working together
	Focus and concentration
FOCUS	Low
ENERGY	Medium
NUMBERS	5+
DURATION	10 min
MATERIAL	None
STAGES	Ask everyone to walk around the room filling up all the space.
	Shout out a number – participants then have to make groups with this number in them. For example, if you shout 4, then they have to make groups of 4.
	Repeat this a few times.
	Explain that from now on, each group is working as 1 body. Each time you say a number, the group has to have that many points of contact with the floor. For example if you shout 10, then in total each group should have ten points of contact with the floor.
	Now join groups together until there is 1 big group working together.

FROM THE FIELD

This is great for teaching children to count, add and subtract.

35	BOMBS AND SHIELDS
OBJECTIVES	Warm up
	Generate energy
	Working together
	Uncover underlying issues
FOCUS	Low
ENERGY	High

NUMBERS	6+
DURATION	10 min
MATERIAL	None
STAGES	Everyone walks around the room trying to use up all the space. Tell the group that they have to keep moving during the whole exercise.
	Explain that each person should choose someone in the room, without letting that person know. This person is their bomb and so they should try to keep as far away from them as possible.
	After a short time, ask the participants to choose another person. This person is their shield and so they should try to keep them between themselves and their bomb.
	After a short time shout 'FREEZE!'
	Ask the participants to look around and to see if they are protected from their bomb by their shield.

VARIATION

Instead of bombs and shields, you could use words related to a theme. For example, illness and health.

HINTS

The group almost always wants to talk about the game and the feelings it produces.

The exercise can produce a lot of laughter or anxiety, especially when participants choose bombs who have coincidentally chosen them as shields.

FROM THE FIELD

This exercise works on people's ability to give and receive attention and trust.

This exercise can be used to generate 'Guardian Angels', a system we use with groups – each group member has a guardian angel chosen by either themselves or the facilitator to help them with any difficulties they have.

The final part of this game was very interesting. I had chosen a shield that had also chosen me as one. They managed to make me their shield and protect themselves with my body, and I was left not knowing where to go because I had no way of protecting myself.

It was interesting to have picked someone as a shield that had also picked me as theirs. On a deeper level, this game can highlight the affinities and lack of affinity between the participants.

36	CHAIR RACE
OBJECTIVES	Warm up
	Working together
	Closing a workshop
FOCUS	Low
ENERGY	High
NUMBERS	8+
DURATION	5 min
MATERIAL	Chairs or newspaper

STAGES	Divide the group into 2 teams.
	The objective of each team is to get from one side of the room to the other without touching the floor.
	Each team makes a line of chairs at one end of the room – with 1 chair for each team member and with the chairs facing inwards towards the other team.
	The facilitator takes an extra chair and places it at the start of each line.
	Tell the teams to stand on their chairs, leaving the front one free.
	To get to the other side of the room, the team step onto a new chair so that the free chair is now at the back. The free chair is now passed forward and placed at the front. The team can now advance again.
	The first team to reach the other side of the room wins.

HINTS

If you do not have enough chairs, or if you are working with older people, for example, you can use sheets of newspaper instead.

37	**CHANGING CHAIRS**
OBJECTIVES	Warm up
	Generate energy
	Working together
FOCUS	Low
ENERGY	High
NUMBERS	6+
DURATION	5 min
MATERIAL	Chairs
STAGES	Ask everyone to take a chair except for 1 volunteer.
	Tell the participants to sit on their chairs anywhere in the room.
	Explain that the chairs have bombs under them which will explode after sitting on them for 5 seconds. So everyone needs to keep changing chairs!
	To change chairs, all you have to do is make contact with another player, but you can only do this with your eyes.
	When you have made eye contact, you can exchange chairs with this person.
	The volunteer without a chair tries to sit down on any empty chair they see. When they succeed, a new person will be left standing and has to try to sit down.
	If the group is quite reluctant to get out of their chairs, you can signal by clapping your hands every 5 seconds when they have to move.

HINTS

It is important to play this game in silence as you are working on non-verbal forms of communication.

FROM THE FIELD

It's interesting to watch the rhythm of the group and how the group gradually develops a shared rhythm while they are playing.

The group experienced a lot of different emotions when they were playing: trust, guilt because they changed places with someone who lost their place, synchronicity – all this at the same time.

Instead of using chairs, I used circles drawn on the floor with chalk.

I adapted this game to introduce image work. Instead of chairs, I used chalk circles drawn on the floor. When 2 people change places, they have to swap images too. So the images never change place, the players do. The person who is trying to sit down has to observe the image in the place he wants to get to as well as get into the space first.

The main benefit of this game is that it works on eye contact. In our everyday lives, the way we use our eyes is very conditioned. Eye contact and concentration are basic elements for successful integration between people.

38	JUMPING CHAIRS
OBJECTIVES	Warm up Generate energy Working together
FOCUS	High / Low
ENERGY	High
NUMBERS	10+
DURATION	10 min
MATERIAL	Chairs
STAGES	Everyone sits in a circle on a chair. One volunteer stands in the middle of the circle. Have 2 empty chairs in the circle. The objective of the game is for the person in the middle to sit down on an empty chair. The other players try to stop them by moving round to fill any empty chairs next to them. Players can only fill a chair next to them and cannot run across the circle for example. The group must also move in the same direction – clockwise for example. If anyone in the group wants to change direction, they shout 'CHANGE'. The whole group should therefore start to move in the opposite direction.

39	STREETS AND AVENUES
OBJECTIVES	Warm up Working together
FOCUS	Low
ENERGY	High
NUMBERS	12+
DURATION	10 min
MATERIAL	None
STAGES	Ask 1 volunteer to be the 'cat' and the other the 'mouse'. Ask the rest of the group to form 4 columns. Everyone should be able to touch the person in front, behind and at the sides with an outstretched arm. There should be enough space between the columns for a person to pass through. Ask the group to make streets by facing the front and stretching their arms out to the sides.

Explain that when the facilitator shouts 'STREETS' they should stand like
This. When they hear 'AVENUES' they should all rotate 90 degrees
(facing the side) to make the avenues.

streets   avenues

The object of the game is for the cat to catch the mouse, by chasing him through the streets and avenues. Neither the mouse nor the cat can pass under outstretched arms.

Start the game by giving the mouse a head start and shout either 'STREETS' or 'AVENUES' alternately.
When the cat catches the mouse, the cat and mouse swap over with 2 new volunteers from the columns.

40	ELASTIC EYES
OBJECTIVES	Warm up
	Working together
FOCUS	Low
ENERGY	Medium
NUMBERS	6+
DURATION	5 min
MATERIAL	None
STAGES	Everyone walks around the room filling up all the space.
	Tell the participants to make eye contact with each other as they walk around and to pair up with someone with whom they have made eye contact.
	Each pair begins to play as if a piece of elastic is stretched from one player's eyes to the other. For example, if one player moves back the other moves forward.
	Remind players that they can break the elastic and find another partner to work with whenever they want.

41	PASS THE PULSE
OBJECTIVES	Warm up
	Working together
	Closing a workshop
FOCUS	Low
ENERGY	Low
NUMBERS	10+
DURATION	5 min
MATERIAL	A watch to keep time

Ask the group to hold hands in a circle.

On the signal of the facilitator, a volunteer starts passing the pulse by squeezing the hand of their neighbour on their right. This person then squeezes the hand of the person on their right. This carries on until the pulse returns to the person who started it. They signal that the circle is complete with a pre-determined signal – a shout for example.

Meanwhile the facilitator monitors how long it takes for the pulse to pass round the circle.

Stimulate the group to pass the pulse round the group in the shortest time possible.

HINTS

When doing this exercise with children, use the metaphor of switches trying to turn a bulb on.

Our record so far for a group of 20 people is an amazing 4 seconds!

The group always manages to better its time quite dramatically, which gives a great sense of satisfaction.

FROM THE FIELD

I have tried this game with children, peasant farmers and NGO workers and it always works really well.

I did this with children and it was fantastic. They jumped up and down when they passed the pulse; it looked like they really had electricity running through them.

The group of teachers we did this with really liked it and said they were going to use it in the classroom.

42	TIN CAN PULSE
OBJECTIVES	Warm up
	Focus and concentration
	Working together
FOCUS	Low
ENERGY	Medium
NUMBERS	10+
DURATION	15 min
MATERIAL	Chairs
	An empty can or plastic bottle
	A coin
STAGES	Ask the group to sit in 2 teams facing each other.

At one end of the rows place a chair with an empty can on the seat in reach of the end team members. The facilitator stands at the other end with a coin in her hand.

Ask the participants to hold the hand of the person sitting next to them behind their chair – so the other team cannot see their hands.

Explain that when you toss the coin, the end team member from each team should look to see if the coin came down heads or tails.

If it is heads, the end players squeeze the hands of the team mate next to them. This message is passed in the same way all the way down the line to the last person sitting next to the can. This person should then pick up the can before the player from the opposing team. The first player to do this then stands up and goes to the other end of the line and all the other team members move up 1 place.

If the coin comes down tails, no-one should move – no message should be passed down the line.

If a team makes a mistake and picks up the can when the coin comes down tails, then the other team moves up 1 place.

The winning team is the first one to have all its players back in their original positions.

FROM THE FIELD

The exercise can also be done standing up and with any other object substituting the tin can.

Adolescents love this game because of its competitive nature – even so, it still promotes co-operation between team members.

Although the exercise is competitive, it needs great concentration and co-operation within the teams.

43	FRIED POTATOES 1, 2, 3
OBJECTIVES	Warm up
	Working together
	Building group identity
FOCUS	Medium
ENERGY	High
NUMBERS	5+
DURATION	10 min
MATERIAL	None
STAGES	The objective of the game is to touch the person who is the caller, without being seen by them.

The objective of the game is to touch the person who is the caller, without being seen by them.

Ask a volunteer to stand at one end of the room. They are the caller.

The rest of the group stands at the other end of the room.

The caller stands with their back to the group and thinks of an emotion (fear, happiness ...).

She then calls out 'FRIED POTATOES 1, 2, 3' and the name of the emotion, pauses slightly and then turns around to face the group.

Meanwhile, the group starts running towards the caller – to try to reach her before she turns around.

As soon as she turns, the group must freeze into an image of the emotion that was called. If anyone moves, or if the caller thinks their image doesn't represent the emotion she called, she can send them back to the end of the room again.

The caller continues to call different emotions and turn around until one of the players manages to touch her.

FROM THE FIELD

When we invented this game we thought of a game which Brazilian children play all the time. It really energises the group. We used it amongst ourselves (adult facilitators) and with groups of adolescents and it worked well.

This is a good game to warm up emotions and the expression of them.

I used this game in a workshop on self-esteem. We looked at all the different emotions and how they were expressed by the group, and which ones were really hard to demonstrate for people.

Working with people in situations of risk, this game helped them to find a way to express feelings. It also helped me to get to know the group better and discover possible areas for future work.

44	WHO IS THE LEADER?
OBJECTIVES	Warm up
	Focus and concentration
	Working together
FOCUS	Low
ENERGY	Medium
NUMBERS	6+
DURATION	10 min
MATERIAL	None
STAGES	Ask a volunteer to leave the room.
	The rest of the group sits in a circle on the floor and chooses someone to be the leader.
	The leader has to make slow movements, which the rest of the group tries to copy.
	Ask the volunteer to come back into the room and stand in the middle of the circle.
	He has 3 chances to guess who the leader is.
	It is important to remind the group not to look at the leader, as this will reveal their identity.

HINTS

The exercise requires a great deal of concentration and co-operation. It is difficult for a new group.

The facilitator should make sure that not only the natural leaders take the role of leader in the group.

Some participants may try to sabotage the game by giving false clues – you can decide to allow or disallow this.

FROM THE FIELD

It's interesting to see how the group grows and improves its ability to work as a unit through this game. I have also seen that the group develops a kind of contract with the person who has to discover the leader. They tend to make it difficult for them to discover who it is, but not impossible. If it were impossible, the game wouldn't be so much fun.

Using their experiences in this game, participants were able to describe the experience of being a leader before starting a discussion on this subject.

45	ONE BODY
OBJECTIVES	Warm up
	Breaking the ice
	Working together
FOCUS	Low

ENERGY	Medium
NUMBERS	5+
DURATION	10 min
MATERIAL	Chairs
STAGES	Ask the participants to stand together (not in a straight line) by one wall.
	Explain that the group is now 1 body that moves together.
	Ask the group to follow instructions without speaking, for example: Sit down! Walk around the room! Take two chairs and put them in the middle of the room!

FROM THE FIELD

When I used this exercise, the group couldn't move together from one side of the room to the other. I talked about this with the group and we realised that relationships in the group weren't very good, there were different, conflicting leaders. After this exercise, we were able to work on this problem.

46	MIRRORS
OBJECTIVES	Warm up
	Working together
FOCUS	Low
ENERGY	Medium
NUMBERS	2+
DURATION	10 min
MATERIAL	None
STAGES	Ask the group to divide into pairs (**A** and **B**).
	Explain that **A** begins by making movements in slow motion, keeping constant eye contact with **B**.
	B reflects (copies) **A** as if they were a mirror.
	Remind the group that they should work in silence and not touch each other.

EXTENSION

In pairs, participants follow each other without there being 1 clear leader.

FROM THE FIELD

Some people got a bit fixed on the idea of being in front of a mirror in their bedroom and that wasn't really the point of the exercise. Some people moved their whole bodies turning, rising and falling for their partner to follow. Some worked very quickly, but others worked very slowly and waited for their partner to answer them.

No-one's in command, you have to work together, it's not a competition.

Eye contact is very important. If you don't look in your partner's eyes, you get lost.

47	GROUP MIRRORS
OBJECTIVES	Warm up
	Working together
FOCUS	Low
ENERGY	Medium

NUMBERS	8+
DURATION	10 min
MATERIAL	None
STAGES	Ask the group to stand in 2 lines facing each other.
	Each person holds hands with the person next to them. Remind everyone that they should keep holding hands throughout the whole exercise.
	Ask participants in one line to lead, moving in slow motion.
	Participants in the other line mirror the movements of the person in front of them.
	After a few minutes, the 2 lines exchange roles.

EXTENSION

Neither line leads. Participants mirror the movements of the person in front of them.
Participants lead and follow at the same time.

48	THE SHOE POST
OBJECTIVES	Working together
	Building group identity
	Closing a workshop
	Evaluation
FOCUS	Low / High
ENERGY	Medium
NUMBERS	4+
DURATION	10 min
MATERIAL	Paper
	Pens
	Participants' shoes
STAGES	Everyone sits in a circle on the floor.
	Give participants a piece of paper and ask them to draw or write about a present that they would like to offer to the group. The type of present could be a material object or something abstract, for example, an emotion.
	Ask everyone to keep hold of their papers and to put their shoes in the middle of the room in a pile.
	Everyone should now pick up one of their own shoes and one other shoe belonging to someone else.
	One participant starts by finding their other shoe. They give their present to the person that has their shoe. That person then finds their other shoe etc.

HINTS

To use this game for evaluation of a workshop, ask participants to write their comments on their pieces of paper, which they will then share with the group.

This is a good exercise to use at the end of a series of workshops.

FROM THE FIELD

I used this exercise as a way of the group giving presents to each other at an end of year party. They loved it.

In every group there are those people who have authority or are authoritarian with others, but even so, with this exercise, everyone was the same, everyone cried, everyone had forgiveness to give, everyone had love to give and receive. So it was lovely, rich, profound and truthful, very productive.

49	GIANTS, WIZARDS, ELVES
OBJECTIVES	Warm up
	Working together
FOCUS	Low / High
ENERGY	High
NUMBERS	6+
DURATION	15 min
MATERIAL	None
STAGES	The group splits into 2 teams.

The group splits into 2 teams.

The objective of the game is to capture players from the other team.

Each team chooses a side of the room to be home.

In their homes, each team secretly chooses one of 3 characters:

1) giants, 2) wizards, 3) elves.

Wizards raise 1 arm and point as if casting a spell.

Giants raise both arms above their heads.

Elves stretch their hands out at waist height as if they are going to tickle someone.

Explain that:

Wizards beat giants because they put a spell on them

Giants beat elves because they tread on them

Elves beat wizards because they tickle them.

The teams line up facing each other in the middle of the room with their hands by their sides. On the signal of the facilitator ('1, 2, 3 GO') they take the position of the character they have chosen.

The losing team runs for home whilst the winners try to catch them. Anyone caught from the losing team transfers to the other team.

The game continues until there is only 1 team, or an agreed time limit has been reached.

VARIATION

Use other characters such as Farmer, Sheep, Wolf, or characters related to an issue you are working on.

FROM THE FIELD

Even though this is a team game, there is real competition as all the players end up in the winning team.

This game mobilises your desire to win and therefore exercises your memory, your reflexes, your determination and your creativity.

I used this game with children. They had problems in the group and couldn't integrate with each other. With this game, we started to work on their self-esteem and how to work in a group. They could win and lose together, in a group, and that was very important.

This exercise is about fairy tales, monsters, childhood fears and the wish to overcome them.

50	ANIMAL WEDDING
SOURCE	Boal, Augusto (1992)
OBJECTIVES	Warm up
	Working together
FOCUS	Low
ENERGY	Medium
NUMBERS	8+
DURATION	10 min
MATERIAL	Pairs of animals on pieces of paper.
STAGES	Write pairs of animals on pieces of paper and distribute these secretly to the group: bull / cow, lion / lioness, 2 cats etc.
	The participants walk around the room and begin to take on characteristics of the animal they have been given (without making any sounds).
	Now tell the group to observe the other animals and begin to interact with them. Finally, the group should try to identify their pair. When they have joined with them, they both leave the game, without talking or revealing their identity to their partner. When everyone has found their partner, ask everyone to check that they have found the right animal pair.

HINTS

You can substitute animal pairs with jobs or other pairings related to the issue you are working on.

Generally, at least 2 participants 'marry' the wrong animal, which causes a lot of laughter. For example, in one group, a chicken married a dog!

You can extend this game and stimulate people to think about the animals they are playing: how they eat, how they walk, what they eat…

FROM THE FIELD

In rural communities, we used this game to start some workshops on the environment and citizenship.

This game was used with rural peasant women farmers. Even after the exercise had finished, the pairs made constant reference to each other and seemed to form a real bond. They would call 'where is my little chicken … where is my elephant husband?'

51	HUMAN KNOTS
OBJECTIVES	Warm up
	Focus and concentration
	Working together
FOCUS	Low
ENERGY	Medium
NUMBERS	8+
DURATION	15 min
MATERIAL	None
STAGES	The participants hold hands in a circle and look at and remember the person on their right.

The participants now break the circle and mingle in the room.

The group comes together in the middle of the room in a tight group. Now ask them to hold hands with the same people as in the circle (give their right hand to the left hand of the person who was on their right).

Without letting go of any hands, ask the group to reform the circle by untwisting the knot.

If the group does not reform the circle try the exercise again.

52	HYPNOSIS
SOURCE	Boal, Augusto (1992)
OBJECTIVES	Warm up
	Focus and concentration
	Working together
	Exploring issues of power
FOCUS	Low
ENERGY	High
NUMBERS	4+
DURATION	15 min
MATERIAL	None
STAGES	Ask the group to divide into pairs (**A** and **B**).

Ask the group to divide into pairs (**A** and **B**).

A puts their hand up a few centimetres away from **B**'s face.

Explain that **B** should try and keep **A**'s hand at the same distance from their face during the whole exercise.

A begins to move his hand, and **B**, moving as if hypnotised, follows.

Remind **A** to explore different levels and positions and to remember that they are responsible for **A**'s movements.

After a short time, **A** and **B** change roles.

EXTENSION 1

Ask the group to form groups of 3.

One person from each group hypnotises the other 2, by hypnotising one with each hand.

Repeat until all 3 in each group have hypnotised the other 2.

EXTENSION 2 – HYPNOSIS IN PAIRS

Divide the group in pairs (**A** and **B**).

A and **B** hypnotise each other, by both following their partner's hand and by leading with their own at the same time.

EXTENSION 3 – HYPNOSIS IN A GROUP

Ask 1 pair to begin the exercise '**Hypnosis**' in the middle of the room.

Ask a third person to choose any part of the body of one of the people in the middle of the room. They then enter the exercise and are hypnotised by the part of the body they have chosen, by always keeping their face at the same distance from it.

Explain to the rest of the group that one by one, they should enter the exercise in the same way. They can choose to be hypnotised by any part of the body of any participant.

Continue until everyone has entered the exercise.

FROM THE FIELD

This technique explores relationships of power that go much deeper than those of a workshop, for example, in relation to dominant powers in our lives.

The exercise is about looking after each other. There were moments when I sensed a lack of care, but there were moments I felt I was being looked after.

I really felt the issue of care. I was a lot taller than my partners and I was worried about the comfort of the other two I was working with.

It's not easy to put yourself in someone else's shoes, so they don't hurt themselves. It's all about power. You have to test all the possibilities and know when to stop.

Hypnosis in a Group is interesting because it gives the idea of 1 great body in movement and this body can represent various things ... it can represent a family in movement, it could be a factory in movement, a community in movement, it allows you to imagine a thousand things.

I used this exercise in a workshop about cultural and ideological expression and it generated a great discussion about how we define our cultural values in relation to the dominant power, like the media.

When I used Hypnosis in a Group in a workshop with NGO workers, I realised that for them it represented how small movements or decisions at the centre of an organisation can have massive repercussions to those on the edges. The tiniest hand movement by 1 person could mean that someone else has to run around to keep up. This was a good starting point to look at management styles and decision-making processes in the organisation.

The whole group had to move with only 1 person as their point of reference. This person co-ordinated the whole group with their movements creating 1 body in movement and unifying the group.

53	FOLLOW THE SOUND
OBJECTIVES	Warm up
	Focus and concentration
	Working together
FOCUS	Low
ENERGY	Medium
NUMBERS	6+
DURATION	10 min
MATERIAL	None
STAGES	Ask the group to divide into pairs (**A** and **B**).
	Ask each pair to decide on a vocal sound they can both reproduce.
	In each pair, **A** closes their eyes and crosses their arms in front of them. **B** starts to make the sound they decided on.
	Ask **B** to move slowly around the room, making their sound.
	A, keeping their eyes closed, follows their partner around the room.
	Remind participants that **A** is responsible for **B** and should take care that they do not bump into anyone.

VARIATION

Divide the groups into pairs and ask them to choose a vocal sound between them.
Ask all the **A**s to go to one side of the room and all the **B**s to the other. All
participants close their eyes and cross their arms in front of them.
Ask all participants to begin walking around the room keeping their eyes closed.
When they are sure they have found their partner, participants can open their eyes
and leave the game.

FROM THE FIELD

*Working with people in the rural Amazon Forest, we used the sounds of the forest
and animals.*

*I like this game because it works on trust and safety in the group. It also opens the
possibility to create and listen to so many different sounds and have the confidence
to follow just the one you have created.*

*The group experienced many different emotions during this exercise. Some were
really relieved when they found their partners and felt a strong bond to them
afterwards. It is a good way to form pairs who will work together well.*

54	SOUND AND MOVEMENT
OBJECTIVES	Warm up
	Focus and concentration
	Working together
FOCUS	Low
ENERGY	Medium
NUMBERS	5+
DURATION	10 min
MATERIAL	None
STAGES	The group forms a circle.

Ask each participant to make their own rhythmic sound using their body and / or
voice.
Each participant carries on their own sound and gradually tries to fit it in with other
sounds in the group. They can do this by changing the speed of their rhythm or by
changing their rhythm to fit in with others.
Carry on until the group has created a rhythm pattern where all the sounds fit
together.

VARIATION

To make the exercise easier, ask the group to start in the same way, but their
objective is for everyone in the group to finally make the same sound.
When everyone has arrived at 1 sound, individuals can introduce other sounds to
build a more complicated pattern. Encourage the group to keep the rhythm evolving.

HINTS

You can use animal sounds or typical sounds from a place or region as an
introduction to working on a theme like citizenship or the environment.

FROM THE FIELD

I did this with a group and used it to talk about co-operation. Was it easy to give up your rhythm and adopt someone else's rhythm? Whose rhythm did you follow and why? What are the benefits of having a group where everyone is doing their own thing? What about a group where everyone is doing the same thing? How do we co-operate, but still encourage diversity?

This exercise develops skills we need for co-operation, especially listening to each other and being able to adapt what we are doing to fit in with others.

55	CALL AND ANSWER
OBJECTIVES	Warm up
	Focus and concentration
	Working together
FOCUS	High / Low
ENERGY	Low
NUMBERS	4+
DURATION	10 min
MATERIAL	None
STAGES	Ask the group to form a circle.
	The facilitator or a volunteer establishes a rhythm using the voice or the body.
	The group listens to the rhythm and copies it – in a call and response with the leader.
	Tell the group that the rhythm can be changed by anyone at any moment. The role of leader therefore moves between the participants.
	The new leader should take care not to let the call and response break down as they introduce a new rhythm.

VARIATION

Use words or phrases related to a predetermined theme. Ask participants to introduce opinions or information about the theme that they are investigating.

FROM THE FIELD

I used this game with young people to talk about society's attitudes to them. They introduced phrases representing common things that were said about them or to them by parents, neighbours or teachers.

56	FOOTBALL CLAP
OBJECTIVES	Warm up
	Focus and concentration
	Working together
FOCUS	Low
ENERGY	Medium
NUMBERS	4+
DURATION	15 min
MATERIAL	None

| STAGES | Teach the rhythm below to the group (it is a well known rhythm in football stadiums in Britain and Peru). |

(x = clap / = pause)

$$| x - x - | x \, x \, x - | x \, x \, x \, x | - x \, x - |$$

(1)

Divide the group in half.

The 2 groups form circles as far away from each other as possible.

One group starts clapping the rhythm.

Start the other group from the beginning of the pattern as the first group reaches the third bar (number 1).

Tell the participants to break from their groups and mingle with the other group whilst trying to maintain their rhythm.

Ask the participants to return to their own groups.

Stop the clapping and ask if they managed to keep to their own rhythm or did they cross over into the other group?

HINTS

It is very common for the 2 groups to unify into 1 rhythm.

If the group manages to keep to their own rhythms, try the activity again, this time dividing into 4 groups. Start each group after the end of each bar marked above.

57	**STEALING THE RHYTHM**
OBJECTIVES	Warm up
	Focus and concentration
FOCUS	High
ENERGY	Medium
NUMBERS	5+
DURATION	15 min
MATERIAL	None
STAGES	Ask the group to form a circle.

Ask 2 volunteers to go into the middle of the circle. One volunteer makes a rhythmic sound and movement and the other answers with their own sound and movement. This should be like a dance or conversation.

The rhythm should be constant and not change.

Ask a third volunteer to enter into the circle. She starts her own sound and movement, making it fit with one of the others. She starts to draw this player away. When she has done this, they continue playing and the other player leaves the circle.

The exercise continues with new people coming into the circle one by one until everyone has participated.

58	THE CONDUCTOR
OBJECTIVES	Warm up
	Working together
FOCUS	High / Low
ENERGY	Medium
NUMBERS	6+
DURATION	15 min
MATERIAL	None
STAGES	The group makes a circle.

The group chooses a place or situation that has a lot of different sounds (such as a market, a school …).

Ask the group to think of all the different sounds they might find in this place.

Participants get into pairs or small groups. Each group chooses one of the sounds and rehearses it.

Now, the conductor (a volunteer or the facilitator) stands in the middle of the circle. He decides with the group on signals for getting louder, quieter, faster, slower and to stop.

The group performs their symphony with their conductor.

59	MR PEREIRA
OBJECTIVES	Warm up
	Working together
FOCUS	High
ENERGY	Medium
NUMBERS	5+
DURATION	5 to 10 min
MATERIAL	None
STAGES	Ask the group to leave the room.

Ask 1 person to come back in. When they enter, the facilitator copies everything they do or say. Once the participant has understood that the facilitator is copying her, invite another person into the room.

Now, 2 people imitate what that person is doing.

Continue until the last person has come into the room.

FROM THE FIELD

Participants reacted very differently to this exercise. Some stood doing nothing, others made the group contort into strange positions and others couldn't stop laughing.

It helped the participants relate to each other and to understand how others see them, by seeing their actions reflected in others.

After the game finished, the group still kept playing. We moved onto another part of the workshop, and they kept copying my position, what I said and my gestures. It was fascinating to see this and it went on for about 5 minutes, and participants started imitating other people as well. Afterwards, the planning for the day was completely changed to work on the identity of the group and the relationships within it.

At the beginning, the participants were very diffuse, but after this exercise, they were able to concentrate more and put their energy into the work we were doing.

60	DOMINOES
OBJECTIVES	Warm up
	Working together
	Focus and concentration
FOCUS	Low
ENERGY	Medium
NUMBERS	6+
DURATION	10 min
MATERIAL	None
STAGES	Ask everyone to stand in a circle and to copy the fifth person on their right. They should copy every gesture and facial expression, however small.
	Everyone will be copying someone different. If, however, there are 10 participants, you will have to use a different number, or participants will be copying each other in pairs and that is not the objective of the game.
	Gradually, the group should begin to work together, and the movement of 1 person will be repeated by everyone else in a domino effect.

61	TRAVELLING ROUND THE ROOM
OBJECTIVES	Working together
	Know the possibilities and limits of our bodies
FOCUS	Low
ENERGY	High
NUMBERS	7+
DURATION	10 min
MATERIAL	None
STAGES	Ask a volunteer to lie down and close their eyes.
	The rest of the group stand around the volunteer and raise him up to their shoulders and walk around the room.
	If the group is very big, the volunteer can be passed from one group to another.
	Repeat with more volunteers.

HINTS

This is a trust exercise which you can only do if the group already has a certain level of trust between them. If not, it could be quite dangerous, as the person being lifted has to feel comfortable enough to stay relaxed when they are lifted up.

62	PAIR TAG
OBJECTIVES	Warm up
	Generate energy
FOCUS	Low
ENERGY	High
NUMBERS	5+
DURATION	10 min
MATERIAL	None

Ask for 1 volunteer to be the 'cat' and 1 to be the 'mouse'.

The other players form pairs and find a space in the room with one person standing behind the other.

Explain that the cat has to catch the mouse.

The mouse can avoid being caught by running up and standing IN FRONT OF one the pairs. The person who is at the back of this 3-person line now becomes the mouse and has to run away from the cat. The identity of the mouse is therefore constantly changing.

When the cat catches the mouse, the 2 players swap over, the mouse becoming the cat and the cat becoming the mouse.

HINTS

A good introduction to this exercise is **Ex. 25 Earthquake** as it is similar but has simpler rules.

Adolescents find it harder to concentrate on this game so it would be a good idea to do concentration and relaxation exercises first.

FROM THE FIELD

This game really integrates participants, even through the touch of just a hand. It also builds trust between people and frees then from the distance that exists between them.

63	IMAGE TAG
OBJECTIVES	Warm up
	Generate energy
	Introduce image theatre
FOCUS	Low
ENERGY	High
NUMBERS	5+
DURATION	10 min
MATERIAL	None
STAGES	Ask 1 volunteer to be the 'cat' and 1 to be the 'mouse'.

The rest of the players find a space in the room and make a frozen image with their bodies (like a statue). Ask the group to explore different levels with their bodies (high medium or low).

The objective of the game is for the cat to catch the mouse.

The mouse can avoid being caught by running up and standing in front of one of the statues and making the same shape.

The statue that has been copied now becomes the mouse and has to run away from the cat. The identity of the mouse is therefore constantly changing.

When the cat catches the mouse, the 2 players swap over, the mouse becoming the cat and the cat becoming the mouse.

FROM THE FIELD

Using this with children I told them that they had to be careful with the statues, because if they touched them, they might break. This prevented the statues getting pushed by the cat or mouse whilst they were running around.

With its roots in a popular game, this technique works on equality of roles as

*everyone gets to be both the tagger and the tagged. This makes it different from the
traditional game where the slowest, the fattest, the ones that are 'different' are
always the taggers. Competition generally develops our abilities to confront and
overcome obstacles, however, in our daily lives competitiveness between people
has become more aggressive. A discussion around these points was raised by the
adolescents after we had completed this exercise.*

64	**1, 2, 3**
OBJECTIVES	Warm up
	Introduce image theatre
FOCUS	Medium
ENERGY	Medium
NUMBERS	4+
DURATION	15 min
MATERIAL	None
STAGES	Ask the group to split into Pairs (**A** and **B**).

Explain that each pair is going to count to 3, by alternating the numbers between
them (e.g. A1, B2, A3, B1, A2, B3, A1, B2, A3, B1, A2 and B3).
Once they are doing this, each pair substitutes the number 1 with a gesture.
Then they substitute the numbers 2 and 3 until they are counting in silence.
Now tell the participants to add a sound to each gesture.

EXTENSION
Ask the pairs to line up in the middle of the room forming a corridor:

A   A   A   A   A   A   A

B   B   B   B   B   B   B

Participants begin counting with their partner using their sounds and gestures.
The first pair stops counting and walk down the corridor, watching and listening.
When they have reached the other end, they join the line and begin counting again.
Continue until everyone has walked down the corridor.

FROM THE FIELD
This takes a lot of concentration.

*I was interested in the diversity of sounds and movement. It stimulated everyone's
creativity. The sounds and movements were very different.*

I found it difficult to express myself with spontaneous movements like this.

*We found it difficult to get away from everyday gestures. We don't make expansive
gestures, we don't use our bodies as we could. We have to break that more.*

The group seemed like a unit. The sounds and the movements unified.

65	IMAGE OF A PHRASE
SOURCE	Boal, Augusto (1992)
OBJECTIVES	Warm up
	Introduce image theatre
FOCUS	Medium
ENERGY	Medium
NUMBERS	6+
DURATION	15 min
MATERIAL	None
STAGES	Participants make groups of 3 to 7 people.
	Distribute a common phrase to each group such as:

Be careful!

Thank you!

Congratulations!

Each group has 3 minutes to make a frozen image of their phrase, like a photograph.

The image shouldn't contain any movement or sound.

Look at the images one by one. The rest of the group describes what they see and tries to guess the phrase.

HINTS

It is important to guide the group into describing specifically what they see. For example: 'well, it could be a person talking to someone' is not as specific as, 'it is an old man talking to his friend'.

This exercise is a good introduction to image theatre and the reading of frozen images.

66	IMAGE DIALOGUE
SOURCE	Boal, Augusto (1992)
OBJECTIVES	Warm up
	Working together
	Focus and concentration
	Introduce image theatre
FOCUS	Medium
ENERGY	Medium
NUMBERS	2+
DURATION	10 min
MATERIAL	None
STAGES	The group work in pairs (**A** and **B**) and in silence.
	Ask each pair to shake hands and freeze in that position.
	Ask **A** to stay 'frozen' whilst **B** leaves the image.
	Straight away, she re-enters the image to complete it in a different way; for example, it was two people shaking hands, now it is a person pouring another one a drink, or 2 people planting a tree. The image can be a real situation between 2 people or an abstract image.
	B freezes into her new position and **A** moves back, looks at their partner and then enters again to make a new image.

Each pair continues for a few minutes.
At the end of the exercise ask for volunteers to show short series of images they have created.

HINTS
This exercise can also be done with the whole group in a circle.

FROM THE FIELD
We did this exercise with a group of bilingual indigenous teachers in the Peruvian Amazon. I was amazed by the beauty of the images that the participants created. They were completely different from those which I had seen in the same exercise a few days earlier in the city. What struck me most was the fluidity and integration of the movements, it was like watching poetry. Their references for 'the everyday' were different to mine. I saw images of hunting and fishing and their bodies seemed so connected to the ground they were working on. They took the exercise and made it theirs, expressed themselves and their cultures through it.

67	WHO AM I?
OBJECTIVES	Warm up
	Working together
	Exploring issues of power
	Issue: status
FOCUS	High
ENERGY	Medium
NUMBERS	4+
DURATION	15 min
MATERIAL	None
STAGES	A volunteer leaves the room.

The rest of the group decides what character the volunteer is going to play and then creates a scene in a bar or other social space, for that person to enter. The group decides where the bar is, what kind of people go there, what people are in the bar. Call the volunteer back in. He has to discover who he is (for example, a priest) by the reactions that the group have to him, how they talk to him, what they say, if people are respectful to him or ignore him. For example, if the character is a priest, someone in the group might offer him a chair or act very surprised if he asks for a whisky and a cigarette, or someone might come up to him and start telling him about a problem.
The improvisation continues until the facilitator asks the volunteer to guess who he is.

FROM THE FIELD
This can be used to discuss concrete situations such as the relationship between rural workers and local landowners. For example, a local landowner goes into a bar, and the workers react to him in a certain way, or vice versa.

This exercise looks at how other people see you and how this often defines how you see yourself. So it is a good exercise to work on identity.

68	ABC IMPROVISATION
OBJECTIVES	Warm up
	Issue: conflict resolution
FOCUS	High
ENERGY	Medium
NUMBERS	2+
DURATION	10 min
MATERIAL	None
STAGES	The group works in pairs.
	Decide on a scenario or series of scenarios to work on with the group (relating to the issue you are working on) and distribute a scenario to each pair.
	Explain that each pair is going to improvise their situation.
	The first person to talk will start their sentence with the letter A, their partner will start their reply with the letter B until they have reached the end of the alphabet.

HINTS

Participants concentrate on starting their sentence with the right letter of the alphabet, which means they don't censor themselves so much on the content of what they are saying. Although the instructions are quite challenging, the improvisations produced are often very rich.

FROM THE FIELD

The exercise makes you do a short scene and solve the conflict very quickly. In the scenes you have to see your objectives and actions very clearly.

With adolescents, it's good to help them think about problem resolution. Their parents don't help them do this. But they can learn to do it.

It's a good way of training agility and quick reasoning for resolving situations.

We often think that we can only achieve things by talking. Often, it's much better if you use other resources and don't just talk.

69	HOW MANY USES ARE THERE FOR A BUCKET?
OBJECTIVES	Warm up
	Working together
FOCUS	High
ENERGY	Medium
NUMBERS	2+
DURATION	10 min
MATERIAL	Everyday objects e.g. bucket, ball, chair, watch.
STAGES	Divide the group into pairs and distribute an everyday object to each one.
	Each pair has 5 minutes to find as many uses for their object as possible. They do this by taking turns to improvise with their object (for example, using a bucket as a chair, a hat, a hole in the ground ...).
	Ask each pair to show some of the uses they have discovered to the rest of the group.

70	IMAGE OF AN OBJECT
OBJECTIVES	Focus and concentration
	Building group identity
FOCUS	High
ENERGY	Medium
NUMBERS	6+
DURATION	20 min
MATERIAL	None
STAGES	Ask the group to make a circle.

Participants close their eyes and visualise an object that has something to do with them.

Ask participants to draw or write about the object on a piece of paper.

Collect the papers and redistribute them randomly among the group.

In small groups, each participant makes a frozen image of the new image they have been given, using their own body and other people if necessary.

The group looks at the images one by one and discuss the qualities it has.

Meanwhile, people try to identify their original object.

As participants identify their objects, either ask them to comment on why they chose them or ask the group to comment on how the object reminds them of the owner.

71	INVISIBLE CLAY
OBJECTIVES	Warm up
	Focus and concentration
	Working together
FOCUS	High
ENERGY	Medium
NUMBERS	4+
DURATION	10 min
MATERIAL	None
STAGES	The group stands in a circle.

One person begins by modelling invisible clay into an object. When they are satisfied with what they have made, they pass it onto the person on their right.

The second person takes the object, uses it, then squashes the clay between their hands and makes a new object.

The clay is passed around the room until everyone has modelled something.

HINTS

Instead of an object, ask the group to model presents for the person on their right and then hand these presents to them.

72	WHAT ARE YOU DOING?
OBJECTIVES	Warm up
	Working together
FOCUS	Medium
ENERGY	Medium
NUMBERS	5+

DURATION	10 min
MATERIAL	None
STAGES	Everyone stands in a circle.
	A volunteer begins to mime a daily activity, for example: brushing their teeth or driving.
	The person on their right asks them: 'what are you doing?'
	The volunteer continues miming their action, but says that they are doing something else: for example: 'I'm reading a book'.
	The person who asked starts to mime the action they were told (in this case, reading a book).
	The game continues with the person on their right asking, 'what are you doing?'

73	MOODS
OBJECTIVES	Warm up
	Non-verbal communication
FOCUS	High
ENERGY	Medium
NUMBERS	5+
DURATION	20 min
MATERIAL	None
STAGES	The group sits in a circle. One person goes into the centre (**A**) and begins to walk, demonstrating a feeling or mood (e.g. anger or impatience).
	A second person (**B**) enters the circle and begins to imitate **A**'s gestures and mood. Explain that they can slowly begin to interact with each other, but they cannot speak.
	Ask a third person (**C**) to enter into the circle and to show a sentiment or mood that is completely different.
	C can interact with **A** and **B**.
	Slowly, **A** and **B** transform their original mood into the one that **C** has brought into the circle.
	Now, **A** leaves the circle and **B** and **C** interact with each other.
	A new person enters and the process continues.
	The exercise continues with new players entering and leaving the circle.

74	GRANDMA'S FOOTSTEPS
OBJECTIVES	Focus and concentration
	Building group identity
	Working together
	Non-verbal communication
FOCUS	Low
ENERGY	Medium
NUMBERS	5+
DURATION	15 min
MATERIAL	Keys

STAGES	**FIRST STAGE**

FIRST STAGE

A volunteer plays the grandmother and stands at one end of the room facing the wall.

The facilitator places a bunch of keys a couple of paces behind her.

The rest of the group, stand at the other end of the room (home).

The objective of the game is for someone to get the keys without being caught by grandma.

The players start to move forward.

Grandma can turn round suddenly, and when she does, anyone she sees moving is sent back home.

The game finishes when someone manages to get the keys.

SECOND STAGE

Explain that the second phase of the game is more difficult because they now have to get the keys back home, without grandma guessing who is holding them. It is a game of co-operation.

The game begins in the same way with the group advancing towards the keys. But this time, when someone gets the keys, they have to ensure that grandma does not know who has them.

For the group to win, the keys have to change hands 3 times before they get home. Meanwhile, grandma has 3 chances to turn around and guess who has the keys.

The group wins if they get the keys home and grandma wins if she guesses who has the keys.

HINTS

The game works well when the group works together to fool grandma into guessing the wrong identity of the person with the keys.

The game is a process of discovery of how to co-operate on a task. The group can only succeed (get home with the keys) if they co-operate with each other. If the group does not succeed and the participants are playing as individuals rather than a team, remind the group of this.

If the group still does not succeed, this may be a good point to talk to the group about working together and / or to try more exercises related to group building.

FROM THE FIELD

I used this with young people with learning difficulties to develop teamwork skills, it was actually to negotiate the care of their plants. They were very enthusiastic, motivated and interested. Up to then it had been very difficult to get them to work together.

In the yearly evaluation in our organisation, we used this exercise to look at the way each worker interacts and how we should work more on communication and participation. It was perfect, we didn't need to speak so much, we had concrete examples of the way we played the game to reflect upon.

It's quite difficult to do group work with children with learning difficulties. But with this exercise, the group successfully started to work together – they really wanted to do it.

This is one of the best exercises for working on co-operation and working as a group. It's interesting to see how after a few failed attempts, the participants started to communicate and plan strategies to get the keys.

75	FANTASY ISLAND
OBJECTIVES	Working together
	Building group identity
FOCUS	Medium
ENERGY	Medium
NUMBERS	5+
DURATION	25 min
MATERIAL	None
STAGES	In small groups, 1 person (the protagonist) explains a scene – a fantasy, which they would like to act out. For example, a scene where the protagonist is a famous singer, gets their own house, gets a degree …
	The protagonist directs the scene with their group, until they are satisfied that it is a good representation of their fantasy.
	The groups play out the scene with the protagonist taking the role of him or herself.

DISCUSSION

How was it to act out your own fantasy?

Did your dream come true?

Was it like you imagined it?

Have you changed your dream at all now after acting it out?

FROM THE FIELD

This exercise is lovely when you see people living something that they have always dreamt about.

It helped everyone to get to know each other better. Finding out each other's dreams is a very intimate process.

76	THE VAMPIRE
OBJECTIVES	Warm up
	Working together
	Issue: sexual health
FOCUS	Low
ENERGY	Medium
NUMBERS	4+
DURATION	10 min
MATERIAL	None
STAGES	In this exercise, participants become vampires. This happens when they are bitten on the neck, like in ancient stories or legends.
	The group walks around the room with their eyes closed and their arms crossed across the front of their bodies.
	A soft pinch on the neck represents a bite. When they feel this, participants should let out a scream of fear. They then become vampires and can 'bite' other people to turn them into vampires too.
	If they are bitten again, they let out a sigh of pleasure and become human again. As humans, they cannot bite other people.
	Participants keep their eyes closed for the whole game.
	To introduce the first vampire, ask the group to begin walking around the room. Explain that the vampire is on his way. Make a noise to show that he has entered the room (close a door or stamp your feet). Then, lightly pinch a participant's neck and they become the first vampire.
	The game continues until participants have become vampires a number of times.

VARIATION

Adapting the exercise to talk about sexually transmitted diseases.

Distribute a condom to a third of the group. If the condom carriers are bitten, they make a shout of pleasure and instead of biting other people and turning them into vampires, they give them the condom (still with their eyes closed). If a player receives a condom and is then bitten by another person, she shouts in pleasure. She then gives the condom to the next person she meets, rather than biting them. If they are bitten and do not have a condom, they shout in fear, become a vampire and can turn other people into vampires by biting them. Carry on the game for a few minutes. Afterwards, ask the group if any of them escaped being bitten during the whole game.

DISCUSSION

Did you get bitten?

Were you protected?

What happened once you had given your condom away?

HINTS

There should always be at least 1 facilitator to make sure that participants do not hurt themselves.

FROM THE FIELD

Participants said that in this game, they could let out and reduce their stress, because they could shout a lot ... the sensation of being bitten, the little pinch, transforming from human to vampire and back again ... ah!

With your eyes closed, you can work more on other senses like touch and hearing.

I used this exercise with a group to work on trust. With their eyes closed, the group felt more vulnerable, and to be able to do the exercise they had to walk, trusting each other.

To facilitate this exercise, you have to be quite dramatic and create an atmosphere of mystery or the participants won't really get into the game. If you don't manage this, then the exercise becomes monotonous and without creativity.

77	GUIDED JOURNEY
OBJECTIVES	Focus and concentration
	Building group identity
FOCUS	Low
ENERGY	Medium
NUMBERS	2+
DURATION	30 min
MATERIAL	Paper
	Pencils
STAGES	Everyone lies on the floor with their eyes closed.
	Ask participants to breathe in through their noses and out through their noses.
	Explain that they are going to make a long voyage. Slowly, they can open their eyes and pick up their luggage:

Pick up your bag. Is it a suitcase or a rucksack? Is it light or heavy?
Start walking ... feel the road beneath your feet. Your bag is starting to feel heavier.
There is water on the road. It is around your ankles ... it is rising ... now it is around
your knees ... your waist ... your shoulders ... the water is disappearing ... now the
road is dry again.
(Take participants through a variety of sensations – walking on ice, through mud, the
midday sun is very hot, it is raining and very windy ...)

You have arrived at a wall. How will you get to the other side? Don't forget your bag.
You find a door. Try to open it. On the other side there is a garden. What is the
garden like? Explore the garden.
You find a hole in the ground. It is very small. Your bag won't fit. So, take everything
out of the bag and choose 1 thing to take with you.
Climb into the hole. There is a light in front of you, crawl towards it. You are in a
cave. Explore the cave, there are parts that are very low. How are the walls? Are
they wet or dry? Rough or smooth?
Pick up the 1 thing you kept from your bag. Hold it in your hands and look at it.
Now walk around the room and show your possession to the others. If you want to,
you can exchange your possession with someone else's.
When you are ready, sit down with your possession.

Now, draw your possession, you can draw an object, an impression or related
emotions.

Now either ask the group to display their drawings, talk about them or take them
home with them.

78	BEATING STRESS
OBJECTIVES	Warm up
	Working together
	Closing a workshop
FOCUS	Low
ENERGY	Medium
NUMBERS	3+
DURATION	10 min
MATERIAL	None
STAGES	The group stands in a circle.

Ask the group to copy your movements as you speak.

Do the following movements and recite the text in italics below:

1. Nod your head up and down – '*In life there are times when you have to say
   YES.*'
2. Shake your head from side to side – '*There are other times when you have to
   say NO.*'
3. Open your arms as if to hug someone – '*Sometimes we have to open ourselves
   to life.*'
4. Close your arms – '*Sometimes we have to protect ourselves.*'
5. Shrug your shoulders up and down – '*But, there are times when we shrug our
   shoulders and say – So what! So what! So what!*'
6. Brush your hands together in front of you, then look to left and then the
   right – '*At other times, we look one way and then the other, and ask: What do
   I care? What do I care? What do I care?*'

7. Move your hips in a circle with your hands on your hips – '*Sometimes, we have to know how to move around obstacles.*'
8. Stamp your feet various times – '*Even so, we have to keep our feet on the ground.*'
9. Lift your arms up and stretch your body as if you were yawning – '*And don't forget that your head can always be in the stars.*'

FROM THE FIELD

I did this with a group of 250 young people and it was perfect because it integrated a really big group and motivated them to start working together.

79	COUNTING 1–10
OBJECTIVES	Working together
	Focus and concentration
	Closing a workshop
FOCUS	Low
ENERGY	Low
NUMBERS	4+
DURATION	10 min
MATERIAL	None
STAGES	The group sits in a circle.
	They are going to count from 1–10 (or from 1 to the number of people in the group).
	The players cannot count in the order that they are sat, and have to count in numerical order.
	Anyone can start. If 2 or more people say a number at the same time, then the group has to start counting from 1 again.
	The game finishes when the group has counted to 10.

HINTS

The group will find it is easier to do this exercise with their eyes closed.

FROM THE FIELD

This exercise is quite a challenge for a group and I would only try it with people who had been working together for a while, especially if they were adolescents.

I did this with a group of adolescents, but they weren't working together very well and started blaming each other every time they had to start again.

We used this with a group of child street workers, and they took a long time to find enough concentration. But with the help of the facilitator, that stimulated them to keep going and to concentrate, they managed it and they were really happy to see that they could succeed at a task together.

I was really surprised when we did this exercise with adolescent street workers. I doubted it would work, but they really became conscious of the importance of concentration.

80	LOOK UP – LOOK DOWN
OBJECTIVES	Warm up Working together Closing a workshop
FOCUS	Low
ENERGY	Low
NUMBERS	6+
DURATION	5 min
MATERIAL	None
STAGES	The group stands in a circle. Explain that the game has 4 movements: 1) clap hands, 2) look down, 3) clap hands, 4) look up into another player's eyes. When the players look up, if a player is looking at someone who is looking at her – if their eyes meet – then both players sit down. The winner is the last person, or last pair to be left standing.

FROM THE FIELD

This technique gets people to look at each other, and get to know each other a little as a way of building confidence and non-verbal communication.

This game can be used to make pairs for a further exercise.

81	WALKING IN THE FOREST
SOURCE	Macbeth, F & Nic Fine (1995)
OBJECTIVES	Warm up Working together Focus and concentration Closing a workshop
FOCUS	Low
ENERGY	Low
NUMBERS	7+
DURATION	10 min
MATERIAL	None
STAGES	The group makes 2 straight lines face to face, making a corridor. Ask the participants to stretch out their arms in front of them so that their hands touch. Explain that the 2 participants at the end of the lines are going to walk through the corridor with their eyes closed. Meanwhile, everyone else in the group softly makes a sound from the forest (the wind, an animal, flowing water). The two participants walking through the corridor will hear the mixture of sounds and feel tree branches brushing against them (arms). When they reach the other end, they rejoin the lines and 2 more people start to walk down the corridor with their eyes closed.

FROM THE FIELD

The boys that did this exercise said it gave them a feeling of peace. One said that he had felt as if the exercise had taken him out of the room.

82	THE SHOWER
OBJECTIVES	Warm up Working together Closing a workshop
FOCUS	Low
ENERGY	Medium
NUMBERS	5+
DURATION	10 min
MATERIAL	None
STAGES	A volunteer stands with the rest of the group around them – they are the water in the shower. The group puts their hands on the head of the person in the middle and then brushes them down to their feet. One by one everyone goes into the centre for their shower.

FROM THE FIELD

It was good to use this exercise with a group of young men that we work with. They touched each other's bodies without thinking about it as a problem, and they even asked to repeat the exercise.

83	GLASS SNAKE
SOURCE	Boal, Augusto (1992)
OBJECTIVES	Focus and concentration Working together Closing a workshop
FOCUS	Low
ENERGY	Low
NUMBERS	6+
DURATION	15 min
MATERIAL	None
STAGES	It is really important to do this exercise in complete silence. The group stands in a circle with their hands on the shoulders of the person in front of them. Explain that they are all part of a glass snake, which is going to break into pieces and reform itself. Ask the participants to close their eyes and to get to know the head and shoulders of the person in front of them by touch. They should avoid the face and be careful of earrings and glasses. Participants lower their arms and open their eyes when they are ready. Ask the group to close their eyes, fold their arms in front of them and begin walking slowly around the room. One or two facilitators guide participants away from walls or crashes etc. Explain that they are all pieces of the glass snake and must reform by finding the person who was in front of them. Once they have found them, they put their hands on their shoulders and continue walking around the room. Once the snake has reformed, tell the group to open their eyes.

FROM THE FIELD

This exercise brings a huge sense of calm and well being to the group.

It is important to do this exercise without talking as the focus is on touch.

This exercise is excellent for integrating a group, but I wouldn't do it in a first workshop. I also think it's important to do other integration games first and maybe some other games where you have to close your eyes, such as **Ex. 53 Follow the Sound***.*

This exercise helped to reduce the atmosphere of competition within the group.

I used this with girls in a children's home. It was interesting to see them realise that they lived together but didn't know each other. Afterwards, they commented how one of them had really thick hair, how another has very small ears. They discovered a lot about each other.

I used this exercise with a group who had been working together for over a year to introduce the idea of finding new ways to get to know each other.

This is quite a difficult game to do because you have to be blind, but it becomes very satisfying by the end. Perceptiveness is the key to this exercise and it is really satisfying to open your eyes at the end and see the snake complete again.

SECTION 2

CONFLICT RESOLUTION, POWER AND STATUS

84	ANARCHY
SOURCE	Brandes, D & N Norris (1998)
OBJECTIVES	Warm up
	Working together
	Issue: citizenship
FOCUS	Low
ENERGY	Medium
NUMBERS	5+
DURATION	10 min
MATERIAL	None
STAGES	Participants make groups of 5.

Ask each group to work together to invent a new game without any rules. Ask them to work in silence.

Generally, 1 player will start an action which the others copy. If this happens, remind them that this is inventing a rule: copying someone.

The only way to play a game within the rules is for everyone to act totally independently.

DISCUSSION

Discuss the need for rules with the group. If the game does not have any rules to use and follow, it loses its structure and its fun, and doesn't let us meet our objectives.

FROM THE FIELD

This game can be used to reflect on citizenship and group work.

This game is great for adolescents that don't want to follow rules in a game.

85	THE RULES OF THE GAME
SOURCE	Brandes, D & N Norris (1998)
OBJECTIVES	Warm up
	Working together
FOCUS	Low
ENERGY	Medium
NUMBERS	4+
DURATION	20 min
MATERIAL	None
STAGES	The group makes a circle and 1 player leaves the room.

The rest of the group chooses a rule to follow. For example, answer questions with 3 words, cross your arms when you answer a question.

When the volunteer comes back into the room, he tries to discover the rule chosen by the group, by asking questions (e.g. what colour are your shoes?) and observing the answers.

HINTS
A good rule to start the game with is to answer as if you were the person sitting on your right.

FROM THE FIELD
The group usually tries to help the person guessing the rule by giving them clues. It's a good way of them learning to work together.

The interesting thing about this game was when the group didn't want the person guessing to give up. They helped him by exaggerating their answers. They tried to make it as clear as possible. At this moment, the group was working together and created a spirit of co-operation.

86	TUG OF WAR
OBJECTIVES	Warm up
	Working together
	Issue: power
FOCUS	Low
ENERGY	High
NUMBERS	6+
DURATION	10 min
MATERIAL	None
STAGES	Explain to the group that they are going to mime a tug of war without the rope.
	Start the tug of war with 1 person on each side, then 2, 3 etc. until everyone is involved.
	Continue the exercise until 1 team 'wins'.

FROM THE FIELD
I used this game to discuss power relations between the participants. Some people just don't want to lose, even though it was only a mime. We discussed this to be able to understand better the power dynamics between them.

87	APPLE PICKERS
OBJECTIVES	Working together
	Building group identity
FOCUS	Low
ENERGY	High
NUMBERS	4+
DURATION	10 min
MATERIAL	Four apples, pencils or other small objects
STAGES	Place an apple in each corner of the room.
	Ask a team of 4 participants to stand in a circle with their backs to the middle and with their arms linked at the elbows.
	Explain that all 4 have to pick up an apple each in the quickest time possible.

The rest of the group observes the team. How long do people take to get their apple? Do they start working as individuals or as a team? How did the team resolve the problem?

HINTS

This exercise looks at how individual objectives often have to be sacrificed to the overall group objective, and the importance of negotiation and compromise.

88	CHAIRS
OBJECTIVES	Building group identity
	Working together
	Uncover underlying issues
	Issue: power
	Decision-making
FOCUS	Low
ENERGY	Medium
NUMBERS	9+
DURATION	15 min (plus 10 for discussion).
MATERIAL	One chair for each participant
	Written instructions for each participant
STAGES	Distribute one of the following instructions to each participant (**A**, **B** or **C**):

> **A** Put all the chairs in a circle – you have 10 minutes to do this

> **B** Put all the chairs close to the door – you have 10 minutes to do this

> **C** Put all the chairs close to the window – you have 10 minutes to do this

Ask all the participants to read their instructions, but not to reveal them to anyone. Tell the group to carry out the instruction they received.

You may want to tell the group that they cannot talk during this exercise. If you do this, the exercise will take longer to complete.

Some participants get very enthusiastic about carrying out their instructions. It is important to be able to freeze the group if they begin to get too physical.

This is a game of co-operation. Various solutions are possible. These include:

Putting all the chairs between the door and the window in a circle.
Dividing the chairs into 3 groups.
Writing the words 'window' and 'door' on paper and putting these pieces of paper in the middle of a circle of chairs.

DISCUSSION

How did the group solve the problem?
How did they solve the conflict?
Did you feel that you were the owner of your chair?
Did you use force? Did it work?
Did you follow your instruction?
Did you follow your instructions at any cost?
Does this exercise have any relevance to your life?

FROM THE FIELD

You can use shoes instead of chairs.

I tried this by dividing the group in two. I gave half the group instructions and they had to convince the other participants to take up positions in the room. This developed negotiation skills, as the group soon realised that physical strength or force didn't work.

I used this in a project planning workshop, to stimulate the group to think about how they could help each other to construct the project we wanted, to think about co-operation and the space that each one can cede to the other.

I used this to discuss communication in my workplace. It got the discussion going.

I did this with a group of 17 young people. They tried to solve the whole puzzle with physical force. I had to stop the exercise to stop anyone getting hurt. It's important in this exercise to agree on a signal with the group which means 'STOP', 'FREEZE'. You may need this if the group starts to get very physical with each other. If this happens, remind the group that they have to find a solution together. You could also introduce the rule that everyone can only touch their own chair.

When we did this exercise, we saw what we expected; some pulled their seats away so they could complete their task, others watched, some let other people take their seats away from them. During the time which we gave them to talk about the task in hand, the group came up with different solutions. Two groups agreed to put all their seats together in a circle whilst the other group preferred to keep a few seats themselves and not participate with the others. The exercise allowed the group to reflect on the importance of teamwork and to consider that to reach objectives everyone needs to communicate and participate. The exercise showed some of the problems the group would have organising a health committee; unless everyone communicated, they would never reach their objectives with the community. The participants smiled at the end of this analysis of the exercise because it was a good way of explaining the essence of group work.

89	BUILDING THE TOWER
SOURCE	Macbeth, F & Nic Fine (1992)
OBJECTIVES	Decision-making
	Issue: conflict resolution
	Issue: status
	Issue: power
FOCUS	Medium
ENERGY	Low
NUMBERS	10+
DURATION	25 min
MATERIAL	Newspaper
	Masking tape
STAGES	Form 4 groups. Two groups are going to build a tower with newspaper and masking tape, and 2 groups are going to observe how they do it.
	Give the building material to 2 groups.
	The groups have 12 minutes to build a tower of at least a metre and a half in height.

The tower can't be supported by anything and must have 3 points of contact with the floor.

The observers choose a group and watch the building process.

When the towers are finished, give time for the observers to give feedback to their groups.

DISCUSSION

Did the groups work in different ways?

How did the different group members interact?

Did the group plan before they started?

Was there a hierarchy in the groups?

Did the groups have a leader?

Did everyone follow the leader?

Was everyone involved equally in the process?

FROM THE FIELD

This technique can reveal leadership disputes in the group, and you need to watch this carefully.

I was more worried about the people in the group than I was about the tower. Each one was carrying out a task and I felt that we could all count on each other.

We used this in our NGO to evaluate how we carry out processes as a group.

I thought we needed to dialogue more, but maybe time was the real problem. Some people were leaders and carried on without hearing what everyone else had to say about the process.

This technique allowed us to see the abilities and capacities for leadership in a group of rural women from the rural Amazon Forest and we used this knowledge to distribute responsibilities to the participants for the next activities.

We did this exercise with 42 young people from a number of communities during a meeting to organise young peasant farmers in Chumbivilcas. The exercises allowed the young people to exercise their creativity and reflect on the process of building the tower. It's a very dynamic exercise which integrates the participants and in this case, it allowed the young people to reflect on the organisational process they are involved in.

90	WHO IS IT?
OBJECTIVES	Working together
	Decision-making
	Closing a workshop
FOCUS	Medium
ENERGY	Low
NUMBERS	8+
DURATION	20 min
MATERIAL	Pens, paper
	Balloons
STAGES	Give each participant a balloon, a piece of paper and a pen.
	On the paper, each person writes something they would like to give as a present to

the group, puts it inside the balloon and then blows the balloon up.
All the balloons are put to one side.
The group is split into 2 groups.
In secret, group **A** chooses 2 people from the other group and writes their names on pieces of paper.
Group **B** decides who they think group **A** have chosen. These 2 people move forward.
If either of their names have been written down, they leave the game, collect a balloon, explode it and read out the gift they have received.
Group **B** now writes down 2 names …
The game continues until there are only 2 people left in one of the teams.

FROM THE FIELD
The group I worked with said it was fun to think about how the other group was choosing people, thinking and acting to win the game.

91	**THROWING THE STONE**
OBJECTIVES	Issue: conflict resolution
FOCUS	Medium
ENERGY	Medium
NUMBERS	6+
DURATION	50 min
MATERIAL	None
STAGES	In groups of 5 to 7 the participants devise a story that ends with an image of someone (the protagonist) with a stone in their hand about to throw it through a window. To devise the story, the groups discuss the answers to a series of questions: Why that window? Is the person alone? If anyone else is present, are they involved? What was the last thing that happened to provoke this action? What happened before that? Was anyone else involved? What were the key moments that contributed to this feeling of frustration? Each group prepares their scene and then shows it to the others, finishing it with the frozen image. Replaying each scene, ask other group members to intervene to suggest alternative strategies and actions for the protagonist. They can do this by raising their hands and saying 'STOP'. The protagonist carries on the scene and tries these suggestions. The other participants in the scene must react just as they think their characters would.

DISCUSSION
What happens in each scene?
What is the cause of this frustration?
How could it have been avoided by the character? By other characters?
Would the alternatives suggested work in your life?

92	YES AND NO!
OBJECTIVES	Warm up
	Issue: power
	Issue: conflict resolution
FOCUS	Medium
ENERGY	Medium
NUMBERS	2+
DURATION	20 min
MATERIAL	None
STAGES	**FIRST STAGE**

FIRST STAGE

The group makes 2 lines in the centre of the room.

Each participant stands with their back to a partner and sits down on the floor.

Each pair interlinks arms at the elbow.

Tell one side that they are the 'YES' side and the others that they are the 'NO' side.

Explain that the 'YES' side has to push against their partners to advance across the room, whilst the 'NO' group has to resist and hold their ground.

The only words they can use during the exercise are 'YES' and 'NO'.

After a few minutes the participants swap roles.

SECOND STAGE

Each pair stands up and improvise a scene, but they can only use the words 'YES' and 'NO' and there can be no physical contact.

Choose a specific scenario related to the issue the group is working on.

DISCUSSION

How did you feel when you lost or won?

Which strategies did you use? Which were more successful?

Think of times you have met with resistance in your life. Were the strategies you used successful?

Are there moments in your life when you have strongly identified with the 'YES' or the 'NO' role?

FROM THE FIELD

This exercise is a way of rehearsing those moments in your life when it's difficult to express what you want.

I really like this exercise because I've always found it difficult to say no, and it was great to say 'no, no, no'. And I managed to keep it up.

93	BOXING RING
OBJECTIVES	Exploring an issue
	Issue: conflict resolution
FOCUS	High
ENERGY	Medium
NUMBERS	4+
DURATION	30 min
MATERIAL	Chairs
	String

STAGES	Explain that the exercise takes place in a boxing ring.

Explain that the exercise takes place in a boxing ring.

Decide on a situation to work on with the group. This could be a situation which the group has already mentioned as difficult to deal with, where they come up against barriers.

One member of the group is the protagonist – the character that wants to achieve something (getting a job for example). The antagonist blocks them from achieving this.

Both characters can choose 2 trainers to work with them.

Construct a boxing ring with chairs and string and position the characters in opposite corners with their trainers.

The facilitator announces the beginning of round 1.

Allow the improvisation to continue until a block has been reached.

The characters return to their corners where their trainers can offer advice and tactics.

The improvisation continues until one of the characters has won the match or it is clear that the conflict can't be resolved.

HINT

Ask the trainers to swap sides after a few rounds, so that they can advise the other character.

FROM THE FIELD

You learn lessons about how to plan for situations you will meet in the real world.

I think this exercise is really emotionally tiring for the people that are in the ring. You can use this technique to discuss solutions to a problem in the group or in the lives of the participants.

I used this in a children's home and they got very motivated.

We used this exercise to look at the up coming presidential elections. The women that participated were able to express what they thought of each candidate, and through this, what they thought of democracy, justice, political values.

94	THE GAME OF STATUS
OBJECTIVES	Issue: power
	Issue: status
	Issue: citizenship
SOURCE	Johnstone, Keith (1991)
FOCUS	High
ENERGY	Medium
NUMBERS	4+
DURATION	15 min
MATERIAL	Paper
	Pens
STAGES	Choose a social situation such as a party, where different people meet and interact.

Choose a social situation such as a party, where different people meet and interact.

On pieces of paper, write numbers 1–10 and tape these to the players' backs.

Nobody should know what number they have.

Start the improvisation and explain that everyone should treat the others according to their number. (People with the number 1 have the highest status and those with 10 the lowest status).

After a few minutes ask the participants to line up in order from 1–10.

DISCUSSION
How did people treat you?
Did you guess what number you were?

VARIATION 1
Make sure at least 2 people have each number.
Tell participants that during the improvisation, they have to find people of similar status to them.
At the end of the improvisation, the participants read their numbers to each other to see if they have joined up with people of similar status.

VARIATION 2
Instead of using numbers, use roles in an institution, for example, director, programme co-ordinator, secretary, driver, accountant, cleaner …
Participants try to discover who they are in the institution by the way that others treat them.
Remind participants not to reveal others' roles with explicit instructions such as asking the accountant to do the accounts!

FROM THE FIELD
I am going to use this exercise in some work on the revalorisation of Afro-Peruvian culture, to introduce the theme.

I like this exercise because of the sensation of being less 1 minute and then more, but never ceasing to be a human being. It shows us that we should be treated as equals regardless of our social condition.

95	THE KING
OBJECTIVES	Issue: power
	Issue: status
	Issue: citizenship
FOCUS	High
ENERGY	Medium
NUMBERS	5+
DURATION	15 min
MATERIAL	A chair
STAGES	Ask 1 member of the group to sit in a chair and assume the role of king (or

queen).

The objective of the game is for the king to form a court and for the other players to become part of this court.
The rest of the group sits at the other end of the room. One by one they get up and say or do something which they think the king will like.
If the king likes what they do, then he can invite this person to join his court.
If the king does not like what a person does, he can click his fingers and the person disappears straight away and then rejoins the group at the other end of the room.
If the king tires of a court member at any time, he can click his fingers at him in the same way.
The king does not have to justify his actions at any time to the court.

96	THE BOSS AND THE WORKERS
OBJECTIVES	Working together
	Issue: power
	Issue: status
	Issue: citizenship
FOCUS	Medium
ENERGY	Medium
NUMBERS	4+
DURATION	10 min
MATERIAL	None
STAGES	The group splits into pairs. One of them is the boss and the other the worker.
	The boss has 5 minutes in which to ask their worker to do anything they want. The only rule is that the boss has to ask for things that will make him happy.
	The worker tries to complete each task as well as possible.
	After 5 minutes, the pairs swap roles.

VARIATION 1

Bosses have 2 workers who try to undermine the boss without him noticing. One way of doing this would be for one of the workers to distract the boss whilst the other undermines him.

VARIATION 2

Each worker has their own worker and passes orders to the person below them. People can only communicate with the person directly above and below them.

FROM THE FIELD

I used this exercise with a group twice. Before playing the second time, I asked people to change their positions in the hierarchy. This made the resulting discussion much richer as they could talk about the experience of being high and low in a hierarchical system.

Some people feel embarrassed having to give orders to others, giving tasks, they're not used to giving orders. I felt like this, so I got my worker to do something that they would like to do.

It's easier to give orders than carry them out. On the other side, you have to know that the worker has to want to do what they are doing or they won't do it well.

97	BULLY, VICTIM AND SAVIOUR
OBJECTIVES	Issue: power
	Issue: status
	Issue: citizenship
	Issue: conflict resolution
	Issue: gender
FOCUS	Medium
ENERGY	Medium
NUMBERS	3+
DURATION	40 min
MATERIAL	None

Distribute the roles of bully, victim and saviour to the whole group.

Ask the participants to begin to incorporate the role they have been given into the way they move.

Tell the group that they can interact with others, for example, bullies find victims to bully, saviours find victims to help.

Now divide the group into 3s (1 victim, 1 bully and 1 saviour).

Each group is going to improvise a scene of conflict (related to material being worked on by the group), for example: a mother and father arguing with their daughter about her coming home late.

After the first improvisation, the participants swap roles (bully, saviour or victim) but do not change characters (mother, father, daughter).

So, if someone was a bully father, they will now play a saviour father.

Repeat each scene 3 times until everyone has played each role.

Now substitute the role of saviour with the role of mediator.

Repeat the improvisation including the mediator, who tries to find a solution to the conflict through the identification of needs, causes and possible solutions.

Discuss with the group the qualities of a good mediator.

FROM THE FIELD

I used this with a group of women, so they could discuss their role in society and gender relations. It worked well.

98	GAME OF POWER
SOURCE	Boal, Augusto (1992)
OBJECTIVES	Issue: power
	Issue: citizenship
FOCUS	Medium
ENERGY	Medium
NUMBERS	3+
DURATION	20 min
MATERIAL	A table
	Six chairs
	A bottle
STAGES	Arrange the table, chairs and the bottle in any way in a space.

Ask participants to move a chair, so that it is in a position of more power in relation to all the other objects in the space.

When the group has explored various possibilities, ask a volunteer to place themselves in the space, in the position where they feel they have most power, without moving any of the objects.

One by one, participants enter the space, putting themselves in the position of most power in relation to all the others.

FROM THE FIELD

This exercise gives a portrait of the diverse types of power.

I used this exercise to talk about the different levels of power you find in one space. For example, after doing this exercise we set up furniture to look like a typical office. Then we examined where the main positions of power were in the room. Finally, we tried improvising a scene where a worker is trying to negotiate with a boss. We tried the scene with the 2 characters starting in various positions to see if there was anywhere that made the situation easier for the worker to get what she wanted.

99	INTERVIEW WITH A COUPLE
OBJECTIVES	Issue: power
	Issue: gender
	Issue: family
FOCUS	High
ENERGY	Medium
NUMBERS	4+
DURATION	15 min
MATERIAL	None
STAGES	Two volunteers sit in front of the rest of the group.

The group construct 2 characters by asking the volunteers questions:

What are your names?

Where do you live?

How long have you lived together?

Do you have any children?

What work do you do?

How could you improve your relationship?

As the exercise progresses, the characters should answer consistently (trying not to contradict themselves or each other).

This process allows the group to collectively create characters who will have some resonance for them, because they are built from the knowledge and questioning of the group.

DISCUSSION

Are these characters typical of people you know?

Are they typical of people in your neighbourhood? In your country?

Are the 2 characters equal partners in their relationship?

How could their relationship be more equal?

EXTENSION

Repeat the process to create an improvisation. This time, the 2 characters ask the group questions:

Where are we?

What time is it?

What has just happened?

Is there anyone else involved in the scene?

When the characters feel they have enough information, ask them to improvise the scene.

Repeat the discussion above and include the question: is one of the characters oppressed in this scene?

If the group identify an oppression, you could do further work on it using **Ex. 128 Forum Theatre Techniques** and **Ex. 129 Rehearsal**.

100	THE GAME OF FAMILY POWER
OBJECTIVES	Issue: power
	Issue: family
FOCUS	High
ENERGY	Medium
NUMBERS	5+
DURATION	20 min
MATERIAL	Chairs and a table
STAGES	**FIRST STAGE**

FIRST STAGE

Ask participants to decide on a space where their family would interact (their living room, the beach, grandma's house …).

Ask the group to set up one of these scenes using the furniture available.

The group decides on the number of people in the family: Is it a nuclear family? What does this mean? Is the father present?

When the group has decided on the family, the group distributes roles amongst them.

One by one, members of the 'family' enter the scene and freeze in a position that gives them most power in relation to the other family members. Remind the players that their position has to reflect and be true to their character.

Continue the exercise until all the family has entered the scene.

Now ask the group to move each character in turn so that they are in a position of most power in the scene. Again, remind the group that the character's positions should reflect their character.

SECOND STAGE

Decide on a situation of family conflict (or use material that has already been created by the group in other exercises).

One member of the 'family' takes the position of most power. The scene of conflict is improvised, starting from this frozen image.

Repeat the scene as many times as there are characters. Each time, a different family member takes the position of most power.

DISCUSSION

What different types of power did you see in the scene?

Did all the characters manage to keep their power in the scene? Did they always want to?

How could different members of the family all keep some power?

SECTION 3

ISSUE-BASED WORK

101	ADVERTISING AN ISSUE
OBJECTIVES	Exploring an issue
FOCUS	Low
ENERGY	Low
NUMBERS	4+
DURATION	20 min
MATERIAL	Paper
	Coloured pens or pencils
STAGES	Participants make small groups of 4–6.

Ask each group to produce a television or radio advert for the issue you are working on.

The groups have 5 minutes to create an advertisement which will present some important points about the issue to the audience.

Explain that the advert can use humour and can also include a jingle, music or slogan.

Each group presents their advertisement.

Ask participants to list all the important points that are talked about in the adverts and to add any information, views or aspects of the issue that they feel have been left out.

Write up this list on a large poster which can be pinned on the wall.

The poster represents a summary of the collective knowledge of the group about an issue. This can be used by the facilitator for future planning, as a reference for the group and as a springboard for discussion.

HINTS

This exercise can be used to discuss the problems of talking publicly about sensitive issues. How, for example, do you raise the issue of domestic violence in a rural community? Can you use humour in this context?

102	COLLECTIVE STORY TELLING
OBJECTIVES	Working together
	Exploring an issue
FOCUS	Low
ENERGY	Low
NUMBERS	4+
DURATION	15 min
MATERIAL	None

The group sits in a circle.

The facilitator begins the story:

This is the story of … and how … (related to the issue being worked on). For example: This is the story of Rosa and how she lost her job in the factory / had a baby / brought up her 2 children.

One person begins to tell the story, but can only say 1 sentence. The story then passes to the person on their right.

Continue until the group has told their story to the end.

VARIATION 1

The group sits facing a 'stage'.

Ask 2 volunteers to stand on the stage. They act out the story (in mime) as it is told, adapting their actions to all the new information they hear. If a third character is required, someone from the group should be ready to jump up and join the action.

This variation often leads to the group trying to catch out the actors, by introducing surprising information.

VARIATION 2

Half the group are narrators, the other half actors.

The narrators tell their story collectively, passing from one to another and trying to keep the story as fluid as possible. Their story must be about a group of people or things (e.g. a small town, workers in a factory, a herd of cows …).

The actors act out the story as they hear it.

Here is an example story:

A group of people were in the town's main square at a meeting. They were discussing the plans for a new road.

Suddenly, one of them jumped up. He was very angry because the road would cut through his farm. A lot of people agreed with him that the road was a bad idea. However, there were others who were in favour of the road, as it would bring new jobs and business to the area. One woman explained that at last she would be able to travel by bus to the local market. The road was scheduled to be built in 2 weeks. During this time, different groups met up and organised their support for or protest against the road. The day came …

103	**HOPSCOTCH SOLUTIONS**
OBJECTIVES	Exploring an issue
FOCUS	High / Low
ENERGY	Low
NUMBERS	4+
DURATION	25 min
MATERIAL	Key words written on cards, chalk or masking tape, a stone
STAGES	Draw a hopscotch grid on the floor with chalk or masking tape. Write the issue being worked on in the circle marked 'home'.

Write key words related to a theme on pieces of card.

Put 1 card, face down, in each square on the hopscotch.

A player chooses a square and tries to throw their stone onto it. They have 3 chances to do this, otherwise the stone is passed to another player.

When a player succeeds, she hops to the chosen square and picks up the card on it.

After reading the card, she makes a frozen image of the word using as many people from the group as she needs.

The rest of the group reads the image. What can they see in the image? What is happening? What is the key word?

Then the player reveals the word on the card to the rest of the group.

Once all the cards have been picked up, look at all the images again.

The material produced can be used to continue exploring the theme.

FROM THE FIELD

Generating material from key words helped me find out the attitude of the group to the environment, before we started working on this issue. I was surprised when a group read an image of noise pollution as an image on street violence. Obviously their ideas on pollution and city life were different to what I had predicted.

104	BALLOONS
OBJECTIVES	Exploring an issue
	Evaluation
	Closing a workshop
FOCUS	Low
ENERGY	Medium
NUMBERS	4+
DURATION	30 min
MATERIAL	Balloons
	Paper
	Pens
STAGES	Each person receives a balloon and a piece of paper.
	Everyone writes down a question, comment or doubt related to the issue being worked on, places the paper inside the balloon and then blows the balloon up.
	Everyone throws their balloon up in the air, so they get mixed around.
	The group has to keep all the balloons in the air without letting any fall to the ground.
	Ask everyone to catch one of the balloons, to burst it and to keep the piece of paper from inside.
	In a circle, ask everyone to read out and comment on what is written on their paper.

HINTS

The facilitator can pick up on common themes or questions for a group discussion, encouraging the group to respond to each other's comments.

This activity gives anonymity to participants, so they can ask questions without embarrassment.

This exercise can also be used for evaluation.

FROM THE FIELD

Apart from providing great material for beginning a discussion on a specific theme, this exercise is quite beautiful when you watch everyone trying to keep their balloons in the air.

This was a beautiful experience as people are often afraid of saying what they think, but with this exercise, they did. They especially liked not having to put their own names on what they wrote and not having to read out their own suggestions, but other people's.

105	IMAGE OF THE HOUR
SOURCE	Boal, Augusto (1992)
OBJECTIVES	Building group identity
	Exploring an issue
FOCUS	Low
ENERGY	Medium
NUMBERS	4+
DURATION	15 min
MATERIAL	None
STAGES	Everyone finds a space in the room to work in.
	Explain that you will say a time of day and everyone should freeze into an image of what they are usually doing at this time (you will want to differentiate between different days e.g. weekends and holidays).
	Ask everyone to try and look at the different images around them without moving.
	Repeat for different times of the day.
	Discuss the similarities and differences with the group. Does everyone get up at the same time?

FROM THE FIELD

I like this because it creates a living clock for the group. This allows us to see the group's routine and to see the routine of our own days.

This is good for working on gender. How are women's everyday lives, what they do, how they work, compared to men?

I liked seeing the differences and to identify myself with people that do different things at different times.

I used this to introduce the idea of working on the participants' everyday lives as we were going to work on father–son relationships, so it was a good idea to start with a look at what they did throughout a normal day.

We focused on a specific part of the day, in this case the night time to see how, and indeed if, the young fathers looked after their babies.

106	PUPPETS
OBJECTIVES	Working together
	Exploring an issue
FOCUS	Low
ENERGY	Low
NUMBERS	4+
DURATION	10 min
MATERIAL	None
STAGES	**FIRST STAGE**

FIRST STAGE

The group walks around the room.

Tell the group that they are all puppets. They begin to walk like puppets – being controlled by a puppeteer that controls how they move with strings attached to the puppets' heads, hands and feet.

Guide the group through a series of movements: sitting down, walking slowly etc.

Now ask the group to work in pairs (**A** and **B**). **A** is the puppeteer and **B** the puppet.

A guides **B** through a series of movements and then they swap roles.

SECOND STAGE

Join pairs together to make groups of 4.

Each group is going to improvise a scene related to the issue being worked on in the group.

Decide on the scene yourself or use material already generated by the group to devise scenarios.

There are 2 puppet characters in each scene that are controlled by puppeteers. The characters begin improvising the scene with the puppeteers behind them, controlling their movements.

The puppets have to match what they say to the movements the puppeteers are making for them.

Ask all the groups to do their scenes at the same time and then ask for a volunteer group to show what they have done, or work on the scenes with 1 group at a time.

FROM THE FIELD

The good thing about this exercise is that as puppets, even though they are really directing their own actions, the participants feel freer, without restrictions.

107	INSTANT IMAGES
OBJECTIVES	Exploring an issue
FOCUS	High
ENERGY	Medium
NUMBERS	8+
DURATION	30 min
MATERIAL	None
STAGES	Decide on a theme to work on with the group.

Decide on a theme to work on with the group.

Participants stand in a circle facing outwards.

The facilitator shouts out a key word related to the issue being worked on, counts to 3 and then claps.

On hearing the clap, the participants turn into the centre of the circle and make frozen images of the word using their own bodies.

If there are any repeated images, the makers of these images step out of the circle and become the sculptors. If there are no repetitions, ask for a couple of volunteers.

The sculptors' job is to construct a group image of the word. They can change how different images relate to each other, but they cannot change the individual image forms.

When the sculptors have finished their group image, you can develop this image into an improvised scene using the rehearsal techniques, or other exercises found in this book.

108	THE MACHINE
SOURCE	Boal, Augusto (1992)
OBJECTIVES	Working together
	Exploring an issue
	Evaluation
	Closing a workshop
FOCUS	Low
ENERGY	Medium / High
NUMBERS	4+
DURATION	15 min
MATERIAL	None
STAGES	The objective is for all the participants to work together as parts of a machine. The movements and sounds that each piece makes should integrate into a whole.

The objective is for all the participants to work together as parts of a machine. The movements and sounds that each piece makes should integrate into a whole.

One person starts by making a rhythmic movement and sound.

One by one, the rest of the group joins the machine, creating their own sound and movement to fit into the whole – the machine.

The facilitator directs the machine with instructions: faster, slower, louder …

Repeat the exercise but this time, give the machine a name: our city, today's workshop, men, being a teenager ...

Participants create a machine that shows how the different elements of its title work together or against each other.

VARIATION

Instead of sounds, each machine movement is accompanied by a word or phrase.

FROM THE FIELD

In an internal evaluation workshop where I work, we did a machine representing how our organisation – CENAP works. It was so rich. It helped to minimise all that discussion and opened up other possibilities.

The machine is interesting because it works on sound, the sound of your body, the sound that you create may be primitive, but it brings together a group of sounds and creates a harmony. And by creating this harmony, it gives you the understanding that a body exists, there is a unit.

This is a great exercise to finish a workshop with as it gives the sensation that you have really built something. Even though it's a symbolic construction, this can be very important for people who feel the necessity to see results, products …

We really felt part of a machine that needed all its parts working together to carry out its activities.

109	THE CALENDAR
OBJECTIVES	Building group identity
	Exploring an issue
FOCUS	Low
ENERGY	Low
NUMBERS	10+
DURATION	30 min
MATERIAL	Paper, bottle tops or other material that can be used in a graph on the floor
STAGES	The group divides into 2.
	Each group is going to discuss different aspects of a theme. For example, absences from a course and workload during the period of the course.
	Ask each group to choose 2 experts in the theme (in this case, the experts could be someone who is often absent from the course and someone who organises courses).
	The group interviews their experts about the theme.
	Now, each pair of experts constructs a calendar on the floor to show changes during a certain period of time (a day, a week, a year – depending on the theme). To make the calendar, the groups use bottle tops, stones, leaves …
	Each group discusses the calendar they have created and then creates a short scene to show the main issues / causes they have discovered.
	The groups discuss with each other the relationship of the 2 calendars and 2 scenes to each other and to the theme.

110	PILOT / CO-PILOT.
OBJECTIVES	Exploring an issue
	Issue: conflict resolution
FOCUS	High
ENERGY	Low
NUMBERS	4+
DURATION	30 min
MATERIAL	None
STAGES	The group works in pairs (A and B).
	A (the pilot) tells B (the co-pilot) a story related to the theme the group is working on.
	After hearing the story, B can ask for any clarification or details that they would like to hear.
	The co-pilot now prepares to interpret the story for the rest of the group. They can do this using a frozen image, a monologue, an improvisation, using other people from the group or on their own. They can tell the story from any point of view – that of the pilot, their own, or any other character.

It is very common for the co-pilot to capture a different point of view from the pilot. For example: the co-pilot may concentrate on the perspective of a different character at a different dramatic moment.

After watching the representation of their story, each pilot says if it has captured the story or if they do not recognise it.

These stories can then be used to build a group story around the theme being worked on by the group.

Another possibility is to explore the different points of view that exist in 1 story – especially in situations of conflict. Perhaps the pilot and the co-pilot have greatly different views of the story. Why might this be?

111	WHEN SOMEONE SAYS ... I THINK ...
OBJECTIVES	Exploring an issue
FOCUS	Medium
ENERGY	Medium
NUMBERS	3+
DURATION	20 min
MATERIAL	None
STAGES	In groups of 3, everyone makes a frozen image of a word using the other people in their group (so each group will have 3 images).

To make the image, each person thinks of the following sentence:
When someone says ... I think ...
For example, in a workshop on sexuality, the word might be 'Desire'. So the sentence is: When someone says DESIRE, I think ...
Each group shows their 3 images and chooses one of them to continue working on.
All the groups now show their chosen image at the same time. They can eliminate any repetitions between groups and join images that seem to fit together.
The group continues adjusting the position of the different images until the different groups have formed into 1 image.
The exercise can either stop at this point after the group have read the image and said 'what they see' or you can develop the image into an improvisational scene using the **Ex. 129 Rehearsal Techniques**, or other exercises found in this book.

112	IMAGE OF THE WORD
SOURCE	Boal, Augusto (1992)
OBJECTIVES	Exploring an issue
FOCUS	Medium
ENERGY	Medium
NUMBERS	4+
DURATION	30 min
MATERIAL	None
STAGES	Choose a word that relates to the issue being worked on by the group.

In pairs (**A** and **B**), **A** moulds **B** into an image of this word.
Everyone should work in silence.
When **A** is satisfied with their image, **B** moulds **A** into an image of the same word.
When all the images are ready, ask all the **B** statues to make a gallery.

The rest of the group 'says what they see' and group similar images together.
The group now looks at each set of images. They can move images in relation to each other so that they fit together. Again the group 'says what they see'.
You can develop these images further using the rehearsal techniques or other exercises found in this book.
Repeat the exercise with the other half of the images
Encourage everyone not to comment on their own image. This means that the image can be read by the group and there will be no right or wrong answer. An image is originally moulded by one person, but it may represent many different things for different people in the group.

EXTENSION
Four Corners
Instead of grouping images together, ask the group to choose 4 different ones representing most of the images in the group.
Place these images in the 4 corners of the room.
The rest of the group – still in the image they have been moulded into – move to the corner that they best fit into.
At a signal from the facilitator, everyone can change corners and experiment with another group of images.
Repeat until everyone has decided which images they fit with best.
You can develop this image into an improvisational scene using **Ex. 129 Rehearsal Techniques**, or other exercises found in this book.

FROM THE FIELD
This exercise allows the group to deal with difficult content in a very subtle way.

It's an excellent investigative technique and we got a lot of material from just 1 word.

With young women, we worked on the theme of sexuality and the girls did images of sexual positions. This gave them a chance to discuss without inhibitions their experiences and to deal with hazy areas such as masturbation, virginity, the use of condoms, pregnancy, in a way which was very close to their reality.

This allowed us to look at the reality of the education system in Peru. After we identified our common concerns, we were motivated to organise a self-education circle.

We used this to work on father–son relationships. The images that were created were strong and full of conflict, mainly expressing negative relationships between characters … that's why we asked the group to construct an ideal image of a father–son relationship – how they would like it to be.

I used image theatre in the classroom and it has changed my way of teaching. Before I was always talking, now, with images, each of them creates a scene in our lessons. It requires a lot of work, because at first they find it difficult and they fight a lot. You just have to stay calm.

113	PHOTO NEWS
OBJECTIVES	Exploring an issue
	Issue: citizenship
FOCUS	Medium
ENERGY	Medium
NUMBERS	8+
DURATION	20 min+
MATERIAL	None
STAGES	In small groups, participants create an image of a current news story that is important to them.

In small groups, participants create an image of a current news story that is important to them.
The groups show their image to the other groups who discuss what the story is.
The group chooses 1 story to work on.
Participants identify all the characters involved in the story.
Participants divide into small groups again. Each group makes an image of the story from the point of view of one of the characters.
Look at each image and ask the group to 'say what they see'.

DISCUSSION
How different were all the versions of the same story?
What version of the story would you see printed in a newspaper?
Would your version of the story be represented?
How could you make your views heard? What strategies could you use?

EXTENSION
In small groups, improvise some of the strategies for 'getting their views heard' suggested in the discussion.

114	MAPPING MY NEIGHBOURHOOD
OBJECTIVES	Building group identity
	Issue: citizenship
FOCUS	Medium
ENERGY	Low
NUMBERS	2+
DURATION	30 min
MATERIAL	Pencils
	Paper
STAGES	Everyone draws their neighbourhood on a piece of paper, including the place where they live and everything in their neighbourhood that is important to them.

Everyone draws their neighbourhood on a piece of paper, including the place where they live and everything in their neighbourhood that is important to them.
Everyone shows their map to the group. Examine the maps and ask questions about them. Depending on the size of the group, answers could be discussed in pairs, small groups or by the whole group:

Where is your house on the map (in the centre or in the corner of the paper)?
What did you miss out on the map?
When the paper finished, what happened? Did you leave anything off?
What is most important on the map?

When people live in the same neighbourhood, the maps can be joined together and comparisons made about what has been drawn on each one and how the area has been portrayed.

When the group members are quite different, the maps can be very different. This would be a good opportunity to look at different ways of seeing and presenting the same place.

FROM THE FIELD
People often represent their personal relationship with the place they live. You can see when people don't relate to their neighbourhood, go home just to sleep, and relate better to another place. Or they might not consider themselves from a community. So your map would probably be less detailed.

When I used this exercise, someone drew their house and made this comment, 'This is the house that I bought'. Everyone else replied 'Thank God!' This was a really important moment for him as he could have some status in front of the group. He had quite a low status in some respects in the group. Someone else did a map of the way she got to her house. She didn't draw her neighbourhood. Then she talked about the 2-hour journey she made every day to work, it was more real, more important to her at that moment than her relationship with the place where she lived.

115	MAPPING YOUR CITY
OBJECTIVES	Building group identity
	Issue: citizenship
FOCUS	Low
ENERGY	Medium
NUMBERS	6+
DURATION	30 min+
MATERIAL	Paper
	Pencils
STAGES	Give each person 4 sheets of paper.
	Ask everyone to write the names of 4 places that are important to them in their town.
	Under each place name, participants write or draw an important fact or event related to that place. This can be something historical, traditional, a personal story or a rumour.
	Everyone places their papers on the floor into a giant map of the town.
	Ask the group to walk around the town, looking at everything that has been written and drawn.

EXTENSION
Everyone chooses 1 place on the giant map and stands by it, forming small groups.
Each group makes a frozen image of the place they have chosen, using what is drawn and written on the paper as a starting point.
All the images come together to form a self-portrait of their city.
Look at the images one by one (if there are too many images, ask the group to choose a few images to work on).
Work on the image with some of the exercises below:

Who Are They?

Ask the group to look at one of the images and 'say what they see'. Who are the characters? Where are they? What is happening in the scene? What has just happened? What is going to happen next?

First Lines

Ask the group to decide on a phrase that each character in the image is thinking or saying at the moment the image was frozen.
Decide in what order the phrases are said.
Without moving, everyone says their phrase in the order decided.

Rhythmic Movement

Ask the group to decide on a movement that each character is making at the moment the image was frozen.
Each character makes these movements repeatedly to create a 'machine' for the image.

Movement and a Phrase

Create a phrase and a movement for each character in the image. The characters repeat their phrase and movements at the same time as each other.

Monologue

Everyone in the image says their thoughts out loud – a monologue – for 2 minutes. The rest of the group can walk around the image to listen more closely to a particular person.

HINTS

If the group is already working on another scene, this exercise can be used to see how characters from that scene would act in relation to the mapped town, by trying out scenes in various locations on the map. For example, a scene devised between street children and researchers was tried out in a busy city centre square and in the airport, to see how power relationships changed.

FROM THE FIELD

You could do this to map your work place, the headquarters of an NGO, a hospital etc. so people become aware of the space that they work in and the power relations to be found there.

We have used this to work on specific problems in a community, such as the environment and violence, so people can detect where these problems lie and think about how to address them.

In a workshop on citizenship, we mapped an area of the city that the government wanted to regenerate. Through the mapping exercise, we discovered a lot of new information about how local people viewed the neighbourhood. They didn't like the local church because the priest was an outsider who was very unfriendly, so they weren't too concerned about that building, it didn't seem part of their community. But there was 1 public square which everyone complained about. The local council had boarded up a dangerous building there, but according to the group, this had just made matters worse because a nearby children's playground had become unsafe. Men were now using the boarded up area as a public toilet, so parents didn't feel comfortable about their children playing there. This exercise was the first opportunity local people had to discuss this issue with each other and share possible solutions to the problem.

116	1001 USES FOR A CONDOM
OBJECTIVES	Issue: sexual health
	Issue: gender
FOCUS	High
ENERGY	Medium
NUMBERS	2+
DURATION	10 min
MATERIAL	Condoms (including female ones if possible).
STAGES	Ask the group to divide into pairs or small groups.
	Give each group a condom.
	In their groups everyone improvises small scenes (lasting a few seconds) to show various alternative uses for the condom (for example, using it as a ball, a baby, a hotdog, a razor …).
	The groups continue until they have thought of as many uses as possible for the condom.
	Ask each group to show some of their improvisations to the other groups.

FROM THE FIELD

We used this to discuss the management of solid waste, so we gave the group material which could be recycled (tins, plastic bottles, paper etc.) and asked them to give us suggestions for their re-use. In this way, we sensitised the participants to the issues involved and managed to get the children to actually recycle in their everyday lives.

117	INFLUENCES
OBJECTIVES	Issue: gender
FOCUS	Medium / High
ENERGY	Medium
NUMBERS	4+
DURATION	15 min
MATERIAL	Paper
STAGES	Everyone thinks of a man and a woman that influenced them as a child.
	In pairs (**A** and **B**), **A** moulds **B** into an image of a woman that influenced them.
	Now **B** moulds **A** into an image of a woman that influenced them.
	Half the group freezes into the images they have been moulded into. The other half of the group 'says what they see'. The facilitator writes key words on a large sheet of paper.
	Repeat this with the other half of the group.
	Now repeat the whole process with images of men who influenced the group when they were children.
	Now compare the 2 columns of key words. Do any of the words surprise the group? Are there any words you expected to find in the other column?

EXTENSION

The group joins all the images of women together to make 1 image and then does the same with all the images of men.

You can develop the images further using the rehearsal techniques or other exercises found in this book.

FROM THE FIELD

This technique works on people's personal experiences of gender, but in a very natural way.

Image work is great because you can't intellectualise it. The content is better because you don't intellectualise, you act.

118	THEY CAN'T BECAUSE …
OBJECTIVES	Issue: gender
FOCUS	Medium
ENERGY	Medium
NUMBERS	4+
DURATION	30 min
MATERIAL	Cards
STAGES	Prepare cards with one of the following phrases on: Women can't because … Men can't because … Participants divide into groups of 4. Distribute 1 card to each group. The group has 4 minutes to create a frozen image to complete the sentence on their card. Each group shows their image to the others. Participants read the image and 'say what they see'.

DISCUSSION

What are the limitations that each group has shown for men / women?
Are these limitations based on gender or sex? Have these limitations changed in their lifetimes? Do you think they will change further? Do you think that women and men should participate more fully in all aspects of society? How can we achieve this?

119	THE INCA MURAL
OBJECTIVES	Exploring an issue
FOCUS	Medium
ENERGY	Low
NUMBERS	5+
DURATION	30 min+
MATERIAL	None
STAGES	The group is going to create a mural along a wall like murals found on Inca ceramics in ancient Egypt and painted on city walls in Latin America. Ask 1 person to go up to the wall and to start the mural. They must have some part of their body touching the wall. A second person continues the mural, and as well as touching the wall, they must also have some part of their body in contact with the person next to them.

One by one, people join the mural until the group decides it is complete.

Now ask the participants who aren't part of the mural to read the story from one end to the other, just as if it were a comic strip.

When the first reading is complete, tell the group the title of the mural (e.g. a story of domestic violence) and ask them to read this story, starting at the other end of the mural. We ask them to do the first reading so that the group can practise reading stories in this way, but also to give them a chance to express all the clichés and happy endings that this first reading usually creates.

Once the story is complete, do further work on it using some of the techniques below.

This exercise has been used by many facilitators to work on gender issues. Here is a suggestion of how you could do this:

Create the mural in the way explained above.

Do a first general reading of the mural (as above).

Divide the readers into 2 groups.

Now ask 1 group to start at the other end and to read the life story of a female character (Mary), if possible from birth up till her death (if the mural is long enough). If the mural is quite short, the story can be of a particular part of the character's life. Ask the other group to use the same images to tell the story of a character of the opposite sex (John).

You might want to divide the groups by gender and have women creating a story about Mary, and men creating a story about John.

The groups tell their stories.

Discuss how the stories differ. What were the major events in the character's lives? How were Mary and John's social roles constructed? What were the experiences that marked their lives? How did they learn to be men or women? How did the interpretation of the murals differ with a male and female character?

You can stop here and discuss the material you have generated or you might want to do further work on these stories:

Chose a section of the mural and make an improvisation. Start by asking the group what each character is saying or thinking at the moment they have frozen and use these lines as an opener for the scene.

Explore the scene that comes before and / or after a particular scene in the mural. Discuss this with the group and then ask volunteers to improvise these scenes.

FROM THE FIELD

I did the story of Maria with the girls and each one went and stood against the wall and created the story of Maria from her birth till her death. Then I asked one of the girls to read what she was seeing and she started to tell a story that was very related to domestic life. It was a story that was really related to the life that a woman in the Northeast [of Brazil] has – she doesn't have a lot of opportunity for education. Then I asked a boy to read the mural but from the other end. It was interesting that he started to talk of another image he had of women. That they invest a lot in relationships, that she looks after all the domestic affairs, that she is oppressed by her husband. He made a quite different construction. Afterwards, we reflected on the role of women in society.

We used the Inca Mural in a workshop about drug abuse with young men. At first a lot of stuff related to violence and their day-to-day lives appeared. Then we started to see surprising things that we had no idea were happening in their lives. For example, one of the images was a character that had received a death threat. He got involved with the church and one of the parts of the mural was a boy with a bible under his arm coming out of a church. When we discussed this, they said that that it was something that happened a lot, it was one of the best ways to escape – you either die or you become an evangelical Christian and escape from that situation.

I used this with foster mothers in the [indigenous] reserve in the Amazon Forest, and through this exercise they became uninhibited and broke with patterns that had been holding them. They all participated and the ones in the mural suggested that other people should substitute them, so they could also speak and see the story as a whole.

When we started to construct the mural, I imagined the different paths that we as women take: free, sometimes submissive, sometimes anonymous, but always ready to embark on our different paths in life.

120	THREE WISHES
OBJECTIVES	Exploring an issue
	Issue: gender
FOCUS	High
ENERGY	Medium
NUMBERS	4+
DURATION	20 min+
MATERIAL	None
STAGES	One person (the protagonist) makes a frozen image of their own life. She can use as many participants as she likes, but should do the exercise in silence, without explaining the image to the group.

One person (the protagonist) makes a frozen image of their own life. She can use as many participants as she likes, but should do the exercise in silence, without explaining the image to the group.

When the image is finished, the protagonist enters the image as herself.

Ask the protagonist if she is happy with her image, if it is an ideal image. Then tell her that she has a wish and can use it to change the image to make it closer to an image of how she would like her life to be.

The wishes can't be magic wishes – that means that the changes she makes have to be things that the protagonist could reasonably achieve in her life. We all dream of winning a lot of money, but this is completely out of our control, it is pure luck.

To carry out her wish, the protagonist changes an aspect of the image by, for example, moving the position of someone in the image.

If someone in the image is moved, they should offer some physical resistance, to challenge the power of the protagonist, without making her wish impossible to realise.

Repeat the process 3 times until the protagonist has had her 3 wishes.

EXTENSION

The protagonist comes out of the image and talks for 1 minute to each person in the image (they cannot respond or move).

Another person substitutes the protagonist and carries out 3 wishes in the image.

All the people in the image say what their characters are thinking in a continuous stream of thought for 2 minutes.

At the end of 2 minutes, shout 'ACTION' and the characters in the image begin to improvise a scene with sound and movement.

What was important when we did this image was that the facilitator kept asking the protagonist if he wanted to continue to make the image ideal, because it wasn't complete, it hadn't reached a conclusion. He decided to continue and eventually he got to an image that was good for him and for the group.

I was the protagonist and I was really open to this exercise, but I was feeling really fragile, and I didn't know how to modify my image. Afterwards, other people substituted me, and some people were afraid for me because they thought that the scene had really heavy content. But it was really good for me to look at all this stuff in my life again.

This exercise works with your reality, but also lets you work on your desires.

121	CHILDHOOD DREAMS
OBJECTIVES	Building group identity
	Issue: gender
FOCUS	High
ENERGY	Medium
NUMBERS	4+
DURATION	30 min
MATERIAL	Paper
	Pens
STAGES	Everyone writes their name on a piece of paper. Under their name they write the name and description of a character / hero that they dreamt of being when they were a child.
	Ask the participants to walk around the room and to begin to move like their character. They should think about how they walk, how they stand, how they look at other people.
	After a couple of minutes, the participants can begin to integrate and talk to each other, observe each other, without revealing who they are.
	Write everyone's name on a piece of paper. Ask the participants to think about the characteristics that each person displayed and to write these under their name.
	Ask the group to look at the papers. Were the characteristics on the paper the ones that you were thinking about when you were behaving like her? Do you think you are similar in any ways to your character? Why did you want to be like your character?

FROM THE FIELD

I don't think you should do this exercise at the beginning of work with a group. I think you can only do this when people feel more comfortable with themselves and know their own bodies more.

This works with what a person would really like to be. That's the seed of this work. It doesn't matter what characters they choose, or whether anyone guesses them or not, what is important are the characteristics that each person displays. I've done this exercise a few times, sometimes it has worked and sometimes it hasn't. I think that it is sometimes difficult for people to relax into this exercise, they feel a bit uncomfortable about it.

122	FAMILY MEMBERS
OBJECTIVES	Issue: family
FOCUS	Low
ENERGY	Medium
NUMBERS	8+
DURATION	10 min
MATERIAL	Cards with family member names on them
STAGES	Prepare family member cards which, when put together make up family sets. Think up as many different types of family as you can. For example, mother and daughter / father, mother and son / grandmother and granddaughter …
	Distribute 1 card to each participant. Ask them not to show their card to the others.
	Explain that when you shout 'FAMILY REUNION', participants have 2 minutes to form a family with other people in the group.
	Redistribute the cards and repeat the exercise.

DISCUSSION

What different types of family did the group form?

When you were doing the exercise, who were you looking for? Did you find them?

Did you end up in the type of family you were expecting?

Is your own family represented here?

123	TV NEWS
OBJECTIVES	Exploring an issue
FOCUS	High
ENERGY	Medium
NUMBERS	10+
DURATION	20 min
MATERIAL	None
STAGES	This exercise is an improvisation – nothing is co-ordinated by the participants beforehand.
	Ask 2 participants to play the newsreaders, one to be the reporter in the field, one to play an expert and 3 floating actors to take the role of any other characters.
	Explain that the presenters should introduce the programme, improvising the contents of the programme as they go along.
	The presenters introduce the 'in-the-field reporter', saying where he is and who he is interviewing. The reporter then begins his interview (the floating actors play the interviewees).
	At the end of the interview, the reporter hands back to the studio, where the presenters interview the expert.
	The field reporter is then invited to ask for comments or questions from 'people in the street' (the audience).
	The improvisation closes when the presenters close the programme and say goodbye.

124	THE EXPERT
OBJECTIVES	Exploring an issue
FOCUS	High
ENERGY	Low
NUMBERS	5+
DURATION	20 min
MATERIAL	None
STAGES	Ask 3 volunteers to sit in the middle of the room.
	The 3 volunteers are going to work as 1 person – the expert.
	The facilitator presents the expert to the rest of the group.
	Begin by asking the expert his or her name.
	The 3 volunteers answer with 1 word each.
	For example: My – name – is – Mr – Felix.
	Ask the expert how long he has been interested in his subject.
	Again, the 3 players answer as one, taking 1 word each.
	Invite the group to ask the expert questions about the issue being discussed.
	When the expert has answered the group's questions, ask the group to review the answers. Are they accurate? Is the expert really an expert?

HINTS

If the group is very large, split off into smaller groups each with their own expert.

125	WHAT DOES THE SCENE NEED?
OBJECTIVES	Exploring an issue
FOCUS	High
ENERGY	Medium
NUMBERS	5+
DURATION	30 min
MATERIAL	None
STAGES	Ask 1 participant to begin improvising a scene.
	When another participant recognises the scene they can shout, 'FREEZE'.
	The scene is frozen and the second person enters the scene.
	At a signal from the facilitator, the 2 players now continue the improvisation.
	For example, the first actor enters. They are reading. The second actor enters as a teacher, their classmate, their mother …
	After a short time, freeze the scene again and ask, 'What does this scene need?' 'What is missing from this scene?'
	Invite suggestions from the rest of the group. Ask participants to add 1 more character to the scene. Ask the character their name, who they are, how they relate to the other characters.
	Repeat this process until the group decides that the scene is complete.

HINTS

This exercise gradually constructs a scenario and its characters little by little. The group creates a scene together.

We like this exercise because it allowed the children to show their ingenuity and to let their feelings flow.

126	LETTER TO AN ALIEN
OBJECTIVES	Exploring an issue
FOCUS	Low
ENERGY	Low
NUMBERS	4+
DURATION	35 min
MATERIAL	A4 paper
	Pens
STAGES	Choose a theme to work on for example: 'How to facilitate a workshop.'
	Stick pieces of paper around the room – each one with a different letter of the alphabet written on it.
	You could use the letters that make up a key word of the issue you are working on.
	Ask the participants to write 1 word on each piece of paper related to the issue on which you are working. The word should begin with the letter written on the piece of paper.
	The group splits into small groups. Give each group one of the pieces of paper. Explain that each group is going to write a letter to an alien. In this letter, they are going to explain the subject of the workshop to the alien (in this case, how to facilitate a workshop).
	In their letters, each group has to use the words on their paper, in the order they are written.
	Give each group 10 minutes to write their letter.
	When the letters are finished, each group reads their letter to the others.

FROM THE FIELD

There was an election to participate in 'Vivendo' – a national meeting for people living with HIV and AIDS, and before the election, I used this technique to work on the necessary characteristics to participate in the meeting – what characteristics someone should have to represent the institution at events. So, we wrote the letters v-i-v-e-n-d-o on paper, and the group started to write characteristics beginning with the letters, and then they wrote the letters. It was great because they created the criteria for participating and, at the election, there was none of that story of men voting for men and women voting for women. This was a great achievement for me, because in all these years of ASAS [NGO] it seems that this was the first time this had happened, I mean that men had voted women and women on men, and the criteria were created from this technique. It wasn't me that created it, it wasn't the institution, it was the group.

The boys made a lot of interesting comments about this exercise: "It made me feel peaceful", "It seemed as if I wasn't here in the room". Things like that.

127	QUESTION AND ANSWER
OBJECTIVES	Exploring an issue
	Building a character
FOCUS	High
ENERGY	Medium
NUMBERS	3+
DURATION	10 min
MATERIAL	None
STAGES	This exercise can be used to invent entirely new characters or to develop existing characters from a scene already being worked on.

A volunteer sits down and takes on the role of a character.
The rest of the group interviews him. They can ask any question they want for example: where do you live? what's your biggest fear? what is your relationship with your mother? when and where did you last go on holiday?
The volunteer always answers as the character, not as themselves.

128	FORUM THEATRE
SOURCE	Boal, Augusto (1992)
OBJECTIVE	Exploring an issue
	Reflecting on and debating problems relating to specific issues
FOCUS	Low
ENERGY	Medium
NUMBERS	3+
DURATION	2 hours+
MATERIAL	None
STAGES	The principle of Forum Theatre is to:

Transform the spectator into protagonist and through this transformation, transform society and not just interpret it.

Through a rehearsed scene (the Anti-model), a situation of oppression is shown and discussed with an audience. The audience intervenes in the action to try to change the outcome of the scene for the main character. The emphasis is on reflection and debate and not necessarily on finding concrete answers to concrete problems.

First You Need an Anti-model
An anti-model is a scene that shows a central character (a protagonist) who is oppressed. For example, a wheelchair user with disabilities who is often late for school and misses classes because of insufficient transport arrangements. The scene also needs an antagonist who embodies and maintains the oppression. The antagonist has a conflict of interests with the protagonist.

The scene ends without the protagonist achieving what he wants. There should be room for intervention from the spect-actors to change the outcome to a positive one. So, for example, the protagonist can't die in the scene or there would be no room for intervention at all!

The oppression cannot be based on physical violence, because it is almost impossible to find ways of triumphing over this kind of oppression without advocating risking your life.

Two Ways to Create an Anti-model

Image of an Oppression
In small groups, participants think about the issue and create an image to show how they relate to it.
Look at the images one by one. Ask each person to add movement to their part of the image.
Ask the other groups to 'say what they see'.
Now ask each person to speak their character's thoughts out loud for 2 minutes (a monologue). Everyone in the image does this at the same time.
Using this material, each group now goes away and constructs their anti-model.

Pyramid Stories
Decide on an issue to work on.
In pairs, everyone tells a personal story (about themselves or someone they closely identify with) related to the theme and in which they experienced oppression. Each pair chooses one of the stories or creates a new story from elements of both.
Two pairs come together and repeat the process, telling their 2 stories and choosing one of them.
Repeat the process if you want to work with larger groups.
Now ask each group to make 3 images of their story – one for the beginning, one for the middle and one for the end.
The other groups 'say what they see'. Explain that groups can change and adapt their stories to include ideas from this exercise.
Each group now improvises using their images to create a scene.

The anti-model can be rehearsed using many different exercises (see below).

Presenting Forum Theatre
A piece of Forum Theatre needs the following people:

1. The actors in the anti-model

2. The joker (facilitator) who:
Presents the actors and the play to the spect-actors.
Encourages and acknowledges interventions.
Supervises interventions in scenes, but does not influence or manipulate either the spect-actors or their interventions. The spect-actors have the final say about all decisions, and the joker should always refer to them.

3. The spect-actors
There are no spectators in Forum Theatre, there are spect-actors.
Spect-actors look for alternative ways for the protagonist to change the outcome of the scene. These can be given as suggestions to the protagonist or a spect-actor can take on the role of protagonist themselves to try out their intervention.
Spect-actors can only intervene in the actions of the protagonist, not other characters.

4. Antagonist
When interventions are made, the antagonist should try to continue to oppress the protagonist, staying true to their character.

Steps in Presenting Forum Theatre

The joker explains to the audience what is going to happen and does a warm-up game with them. You can adapt some of the exercises from the first section of this manual for use with a seated audience.

The scene is played.

The joker then asks the spect-actors to identify the protagonist and the oppression. The scene is played for a second time (or if the scene is very long, the spect-actors decide on which part of the scene they want to work on).

At any moment, a spect-actor can put up their hand and shout 'STOP'.

The joker then asks them for their name and to describe their intervention – how they think the protagonist can change the outcome of the scene. Their suggestion cannot contain any magic. The suggestion has to be something that the protagonist could reasonably achieve without relying on extraordinary luck or changes in fortune, such as winning the lottery.

The joker encourages the spect-actor to try out their intervention by taking the role of the protagonist. If they really don't want to, then the actor already playing the protagonist can try out the suggestion.

Other actors in the scene stay true to their characters. They should only modify their attitudes and actions if they feel that the intervention would make their character do so.

The facilitator gives enough time for the intervention to be tried and then asks the spect-actors whether or not the intervention has been successful. Did the protagonist get what she originally wanted? Did the intervention use any magic?

The joker then invites more interventions either for the same part of the scene or for a fresh part.

The interventions continue until a number of different interventions have been successful or until time runs out.

FROM THE FIELD

We did Forum Theatre with a group of fathers. The subject was unwanted pregnancy. It created an atmosphere of freedom in which to change behaviour – and not just of the protagonist on stage. It was no fantasy!

REHEARSAL TECHNIQUES

1. TALKING WITH NUMBERS

The actors substitute the dialogue with numbers from 1–10.

2. PLAY TO THE DEAF

The scene is played without any words. The characters don't use mime or exaggerate gestures, but play the scene as though the sound has been turned down. After watching the scene, ask the rest of the group to tell the story as they understand it. The actors will be able to see if any part of the story is unclear without words. This exercise helps the group to identify key moments and any superfluous action in the scene.

3. STOP AND THINK

During the scene, the facilitator shouts 'STOP AND THINK'. All the actors then freeze and say their character's thoughts out loud. The facilitator then shouts

'CONTINUE'. This exercise helps the actors to understand their motivations for action.

VARIATION
The facilitator stops the action and asks 1 particular character 'what are you thinking now?' The actor responds in character and tells the rest of the group what the character is thinking. Then the scene continues.

4. INTERVIEW
In character, 1 actor sits in front of the group who asks the character questions about their life, their likes and dislikes, what they think of the other characters and how they understand the scene.

5. JUST 1 FEELING
Rehearse the scene using only 1 emotion, love or impatience for example, even if this seems to contradict the action in the scene. This exercise helps the actors to discover subtle emotions in a scene, which often surprise them.

6. IN THE STYLE OF ...
Decide on a style of performance from theatre or television, for example: circus, Mexican soap opera, western, silent film, opera …
Rehearse the scene in this style without changing the text or emotional motivation of the scene.

7. RASHOMON
One character creates an image using the other characters, to show their subjective view of the scene.
The scene is now rehearsed without anyone moving from their position in the image.
The characters maintain the original text and relationships, but can adjust their emotions according to their position in the image (e.g. standing on a table over everyone else or isolated from the rest of the group).

8. INVISIBLE CHARACTER
Rehearse the scene without one of the characters. The actors play the scene as if that character were there, dialoguing with him and leaving a space where his words would be.
This technique lets actors see the other characters with more clarity – they have to strongly imagine and visualise words that are not said and gestures that are not made.

9. BEFORE AND AFTER
Improvise the scenes that would have happened before and after the anti-model. This gives the actors knowledge of how they have arrived in the situation they are in and what the consequences will be.

10. SPEED RUN
Rehearse the scene as quickly and with as much energy as possible. No lines or actions should be cut.

11. SLOW MOTION

Rehearse the scene in slow motion without leaving out any dialogue or action.

12. LARGER THAN LIFE

The actors magnify all their emotions, movements, conflicts etc. as much as possible. They should not worry about staying within the bounds of realism. For example, a character that hates should hate with their heart and soul, a character who shouts should exaggerate their shout as much as they can.

13. CHANGING CHARACTERS

The actors exchange characters with each other and then rehearse the scene (especially those characters who have a relationship e.g. husband and wife, father and son, boss and worker). The actors don't have to learn each other's lines, just give a general idea of the character and the action.

SECTION 4

EVALUATION

130	FEARS AND EXPECTATIONS REVIEW
OBJECTIVES	Evaluation (of hopes and fears)
FOCUS	Low
ENERGY	Low
NUMBERS	2+
DURATION	10 min
MATERIAL	Paper, stickers
STAGES	At the end of the workshop or series of workshops, review the list of fears and expectations the group produced at the beginning. Turn the fears into positive sentences. For example: 'I might be late', becomes 'I arrived on time'. 'I won't be able to use the things I learnt in the workshop' becomes 'the workshop will help me in my life'. On a large piece of paper, draw 5 columns. In the first one, list the hopes and translated fears. Across the top of the other columns, draw 4 faces ranging from a very happy one in the first column to a very sad one in the last. For each hope or fear, participants place a sticker in the box that shows to what degree the hope / fear has been realised.

131	FOLLOW THE LEADER
OBJECTIVES	Working together Evaluation Closing a workshop
FOCUS	Low
ENERGY	High
NUMBERS	4+
DURATION	10 min
MATERIAL	None
STAGES	The group makes 2 lines, one on each side of the room. Ask the first person in each line – the leader – to think of a movement and sound that represent an important moment in today's workshop. The rest of the line copies the leader and begins walking in line around the room. When the facilitator shouts 'CHANGE', the leader goes to the back of their line and a new leader thinks of their own movement and sound.

Use the exercise as a warm up by asking the participants to think of any movement and sound.
You could also do this exercise with taped or live music. In this case, it will be a warm-up exercise, as the group will respond to the mood of the music.

FROM THE FIELD
This is a creative and energetic way to end a workshop, especially if you've been dealing with heavy issues.

132	GRAFFITI WALL
OBJECTIVES	Evaluation
FOCUS	Low
ENERGY	Low
NUMBERS	4+
DURATION	Throughout the workshop
MATERIAL	Large pieces of paper
	Pens
STAGES	Pin a large piece of paper onto the wall at the beginning of the workshop.
	Explain to the group that at any time during the workshop, without interrupting an exercise, they can go up to the graffiti wall and write or draw their comments, observations, feelings or messages to or from the group.

HINTS
This evaluation exercise collects information throughout a process rather than at the end. It allows the facilitator to respond to criticisms, doubts or questions as they arise.

FROM THE FIELD
I use this technique quite a lot and I have found that the comments get more personal as time goes on. In the first week, there are a lot of quotes and simple drawings of flowers, the sun, that kind of thing. Gradually over the days, the messages change. By the end there is everything from expressions of deep emotions, evaluative comments on the workshop, invites to parties, apologies for absences, everything you could imagine. During one workshop, an incident occurred involving a young man who was accused of invading the personal space of a woman participant. Although I thought we had dealt with the issue in the workshop, a conversation about the incident developed on the graffiti wall, so I knew that the situation hadn't been resolved.

This is an important means of communication and works as a kind of thermometer of the group's feelings in relation to the workshop.

133	THE PRESENT
OBJECTIVES	Evaluation
	Working together
FOCUS	High
ENERGY	Medium

NUMBERS	4+
DURATION	20 min
MATERIAL	None
STAGES	Everyone sits in a circle. One person thinks of a present that they would like to give to the person on their right. The present can be an object, an emotion or something else related to the workshop.
	They then give the present to the person on their right either using words or mime. The exercise continues around the circle.

FROM THE FIELD

I did this with adolescent girls that were having a lot of problems relating to each other. The exercise closed the day and was a moment of reconciliation for them.

There are some people in the group who have a relationship of authority, of authoritarianism over the others, but at this moment, with this exercise, everyone was equal, everyone cried, everyone had forgiveness to give and to receive. It was beautiful, rich, deep and truthful, very productive.

134	PHOTOS
OBJECTIVES	Evaluation
FOCUS	Low
ENERGY	Medium
NUMBERS	4+
DURATION	Throughout the workshop
MATERIAL	Camera and films
	Paper
	Pens
STAGES	Explain to the group that during all workshops, participants will have access to a camera.
	They should feel free to take photos of any moment they think is important in the workshop.
	Set a limit of photos that can be taken in 1 session.
	It might take the group a couple of sessions to get used to using the camera and to remember it is there.
	After a few sessions, or before the final one, develop the photos and ask the group to choose between 10 and 20 of them.
	Place these photos on sheets of paper. Now ask everyone to write a comment under each photo explaining why the image is important, what it reminds them of, what was happening at this moment …
	You might want to make an exhibition of all the photos and perhaps the comments for other people to see.

HINTS

When we are evaluating workshops, we are constantly looking for ways to facilitate evaluations that come from the participant. Using photos takes the idea of observation 1 step further. Photographs show us the observations of the participants, what they see. It is their gaze.

Using photos systematically throughout a series of workshops can reveal the group's perception of the workshop process. The photos illustrate key moments as understood by the participants and not by the facilitator.

The first time I used a camera with a group, they didn't want to go near it. In the second session, they asked me to take photos for them. Gradually a couple in the group started to take 1 or 2. Then it turned into an avalanche. I had to limit the number of pictures they could take! When they were developed, I was quite surprised at some of the moments they had decided to photograph – there were a lot of pictures of the group laughing and generally messing about. I think this was one of the most important points about participating in the workshops for them – the chance to have a laugh, to work together as a group. I hadn't realised this before.

135	PAPIER-MÂCHÉ
OBJECTIVES	Exploring an issue
	Evaluation
	Closing a workshop
FOCUS	Medium
ENERGY	Medium
NUMBERS	4+
DURATION	15 min
MATERIAL	Newspaper
	Masking tape
	Scissors
STAGES	Form small groups of 4–6 people. Each group chooses person to be the model.
	Each group is going to create a papier-mâché sculpture using their model, newspapers, masking tape and scissors.
	The sculptures are an evaluation of the workshop for each group.
	Give the groups 10 minutes to finish their sculptures. Then ask the groups to present their sculpture to the other groups and to explain what they have created and why.

HINTS

Use the same exercise to research a theme with a group. For example, with NGO workers in the Andes in Peru, I asked groups to make sculptures of Andean man and Andean woman. Each group then explained their sculpture. The participants then began a discussion of stereotypes, gender roles and the image that Andean people had in other parts of the country.

FROM THE FIELD

I am always surprised when I use this exercise at the inventive and beautiful sculptures that people can produce in 10 minutes.

136	POSTCARD
OBJECTIVES	Evaluation
	Closing a workshop
FOCUS	Low
ENERGY	Low
NUMBERS	2+

DURATION	10 min
MATERIAL	Paper
STAGES	Everyone in the group writes a postcard to evaluate the day's workshop.
	Give everyone a blank piece of paper.
	One side of the paper is for drawing and the other writing.
	Both the drawing and text should express an opinion or feelings about that day's workshop.
	Collect up all the postcards and distribute them among the group. Ask everyone to read out the postcard they have received.

HINTS

Ask everyone to write a postcard to the person sitting next to them.

FROM THE FIELD

I used this exercise to end the work we were doing and it produced strong opinions and a very supportive atmosphere: one of the girls had argued with the group earlier as they had accused her of being selfish and not sharing her food. This had made her cry, but when they wrote the postcards, nearly all of them sent her one with a message of support.

137	**EVALUATION A, B, C**
OBJECTIVES	Evaluation
FOCUS	Low
ENERGY	Low
NUMBERS	4+
DURATION	15 min
MATERIAL	Sheets of paper
	Pencils
STAGES	Stick pieces of paper around the room – each one with 1 letter from the name of the issue you are evaluating. For example, in one workshop, 6 pieces of paper were hung up, each one with one of the letters from the project title written on.
	Divide each piece of paper in 2 – on one side draw a happy face and on the other a sad face.
	Participants write 2 words on each piece of paper starting with the letter at the top. They write 1 positive aspect and 1 negative aspect of what is being evaluated.
	Look at the words with the group and use them as a basis for discussion.

138	**THE TREE**
OBJECTIVES	Evaluation
FOCUS	Low
ENERGY	Low
NUMBERS	4+
DURATION	20 min
MATERIAL	Sheets of paper
	Pencils

Before the workshop, draw a tree on a large piece of paper. The tree should have roots, different types of branches, some leaves, flowers ... lots of different environments from barren ones to quite green rich areas.

Ask everyone in the group to look at the tree and decide where they would put themselves on it, if the tree were their experience in the group.

Ask everyone to get a small piece of paper and write on it why they have chosen that particular place, then fold up the paper and stick it on the tree in the place they have chosen.

The papers can be read out to the group (anonymously) and the comments used by the facilitator for an evaluation of the workshop.

You can also use this exercise to look at issues. For example, the tree is the political system in your country. Where would you put yourself on it and why?

139	THE STRING
OBJECTIVES	Evaluation
	Closing a workshop
FOCUS	High
ENERGY	Low
NUMBERS	4+
DURATION	5 min
MATERIAL	String
	Scissors
STAGES	The group sits in a circle.

Give the ball of string to someone in the circle. She holds onto its end and throws the rest of it across the circle to another player. She then gives a message to the person who catches the string.

Depending on context, the message can be a comment about the workshop (something she has liked or disliked), a message for the person to take away from the group, a hope for the future ...

The receiver then holds onto the string and throws the ball across the room to another player.

The process continues until everyone is holding onto the string, which has made a spider's web pattern.

If this is the last workshop, ask someone to cut all the string connections between players. Everyone can keep their own piece of string to remind them of the message they received.

FROM THE FIELD

Instead of string, the players can use their own hands. I tried this when I was working on integrating the participants of my group, and it worked really well. They all got really close to each other.

This exercise can deal with situations that were possibly not verbalised during a session. It provides time to reflect on the issues that have been worked on.

When a group is going to break up, this is a highly emotional moment; if each participant keeps their piece of string, it can symbolise everything they have shared during their time together.

140	CRYSTAL BALL
OBJECTIVES	Evaluation
	Closing a workshop
FOCUS	High
ENERGY	Medium
NUMBERS	4+
DURATION	15 min
MATERIAL	None
STAGES	The group stands in a circle.

Someone from the group goes into the centre of the circle and creates a frozen image representing a significant moment in the workshop for them. The image is made in silence and can include as many people or objects as necessary. The people moulding the image decide whether or not to include themselves in the image.

The group applauds the image and the next participant begins moulding.

The group may or may not feel the need to comment on the images.

THEATRE, PARTICIPATION AND EMPOWERMENT

PARTICIPATORY DEVELOPMENT

During the 1970s there was a growing awareness amongst theorists and practitioners that poverty was not being alleviated by rural development programmes. Early analyses of the Green Revolution, which sought to alleviate rural poverty through an increase in crop yields, provided evidence that food production was not a long-term solution to world hunger and poverty. Disenchantment and lessons learnt from this and other development programmes led theorists and practitioners to look for alternatives to modernist development theory that would enable people to manage their own welfare, and in the 1970s many NGOs designed income-generating projects which would allow people to participate in their own development, either by providing services for themselves or by determining the assistance they received from the state.

Participatory methodologies were subsequently embraced by theorists and grassroots organisations alike. Some perceived participation as an efficient means of improving project results: by including local human resources, projects would have more of a chance of success. Others regarded participation as an end; a way of finding long-term solutions to people's poverty structured on people's needs, their analysis of issues and their decision-making processes.

There is still much debate about the terms 'development' and 'participation'. I have used a definition of participatory development based on the notion that members of a community are the best people to identify problems, set priorities, design strategies and carry them out. This process mobilises human creativity to solve social problems and, through the transformation of the participants, addresses the underlying causes of those problems.

> People cannot be developed; they can only develop themselves ... man develops himself [sic] by what he does; he develops himself by making his own decisions, by increasing his understanding of what he is doing, and why; by increasing his own knowledge and ability, and by his own full participation – as an equal – in the life of the community he lives in.[1]

WHY FACILITATE EMPOWERMENT?

For participatory development to succeed, people must be free to make autonomous choices so that they can improve their control over resources, determine their own agendas and make their own decisions. Empowerment is about making these choices and having a *right* to make and take responsibility for them. It is a process by which 'people, groups who are powerless, become aware of power dynamics in their lives, develop skills and capacity for gaining reasonable control over their lives, without infringing upon rights of others, and support empowerment of others.'[2] Empowerment is not just about access to resources and opportunities; it is about *control* of those resources and opportunities.

Empowerment places an emphasis on self-development and autonomous action whilst acknowledging the validity and importance of people's skills and strategies. This approach to development values the experiences and knowledge of all stakeholders and is intrinsically linked with the notion of power and its reverse: powerlessness or the absence of power.

Power is experienced in everyday life and is part of complex social systems. Rowlands[3] discusses 3 models of power which are useful when talking about empowerment, participatory development and the role of Theatre and Development. The first of these is *power over*, which is exercised by dominant social, political, economic or cultural groups over others. To obtain *power over*, groups or individuals must participate in structures defined by those who already have this power. Women for example, may have their goals shaped by the social systems defined by men. Power is a finite quantity within a closed system and if some possess more, others will have less. *Power over* is often fragile and temporary as it can be easily won and lost.

A second model is *power to*. In this model, power has a generative, limitless quality, which suggests that its growth in one person does not negatively affect another. However, it is still based within pre-established decision-making systems and allows people to act upon others. It cannot therefore be used to describe co-operative efforts, where everyone is of an equal status.

A third model of power is *power from within*. *Power from within* is self-generating, a process by which humans develop self-respect and a respect for others as they come to accept themselves and others. It is the acceptance of difference and the recognition that individuals simultaneously accede to and exercise power. The definition of empowerment used here is based on the generation of *power from within*, as this model facilitates autonomous choices and control over resources therefore guaranteeing the rights of others.

Empowerment generates power and allows people to become more aware of their own interests and how they relate to the interests of others. In a development approach rooted in empowerment, people improve their control over resources, determine their own agendas and make their own decisions. This process relies on ways of working which are close to people's everyday experiences and build upon the intellectual, emotional and cultural resources of each participant. This is where theatre can prove extremely valuable in development initiatives.

PEDAGOGY OF THE OPPRESSED AND THEATRE AND DEVELOPMENT

Links can be made between participation, empowerment and theatre through a reading of *Pedagogy of the Oppressed*[4], in which Paulo Freire considered the use of conscientisation for the empowerment of men and women in Latin America. Freire argued that as long as the oppressed were unaware of the causes of oppression, they would not begin to challenge their exploitation. They could not, however, be *made* aware as this would be treating the oppressed as objects in a system of 'banking education'[5] in which knowledge was deposited into the learner's mind as if the student were a receptacle to be filled. As an alternative, Freire advocated a problem-posing style of education based on dialogue and critical thought.

A central idea to *Pedagogy of the Oppressed* is the 'culture of silence'. This term is used to describe how oppressors overwhelm the oppressed with their values and norms, which effectively silence them. Freire also talks of the idea of 'myths' which the oppressed internalise, becoming dependent on the culture of the oppressors, the 'experts' in society. The needs of the oppressed and the knowledge gained from their own experience are subsequently ignored and devalued.

Freire's concept of conscientisation is useful to a development approach whose aim is to facilitate the formation of identity and political consciousness in order to transform the social order. Conscientisation builds people's organisational capacity so that they can organise around self-defined priorities and concerns. Participants analyse and question realities and reflect on strategies for change, demystifying knowledge and constructing their own consciousness. It is therefore possible for people to move beyond acceptance of existing structures although their ability to act will be limited by many other social and economic factors.

WHY USE THEATRE IN DEVELOPMENT WORK?

Many grassroots development practitioners have recognised the rich resource that their own cultural traditions represent. In experimenting with ways to involve people in the development process, new directions for change have emerged which utilise people's communication skills and cultural forms and allow projects to reach those who have had no formal access to reading and writing skills.

Many development organisations have discovered that theatre can be a dynamic and evolutionary tool for change which can facilitate dialogue and reflective participation (see the **Resources for Theatre and Development** section of this book for examples). Development practitioners who are interested in finding new ways of giving voice to socially excluded people have used theatre as a vehicle through which people can tell their own stories, present issues and address real problems.

Theatre-based techniques are useful to any development initiative which aims to build upon the intellectual, emotional and creative resources of each participant. Theatre and Development draws on the specifically human capacity to create and to invent new ways of life and can therefore facilitate a process whereby people not only adapt their environment, but also transform it with their own creative initiatives.

CAN THEATRE AND DEVELOPMENT BE COMBINED WITH OTHER METHODOLOGIES?

Theatre can be used in combination with other methodologies to enhance participation in existing development processes. One such methodology is Participatory Rural Appraisal (PRA): a problem-solving approach that uncovers community needs and mobilises the creative production of relevant solutions. PRA requires stakeholders in the development process to participate actively in diagnosis and evaluation by critically reflecting on their situation. It can take many forms, be carried out by whole communities, groups or individuals and can facilitate the exploration of a theme, research, planning, implementation, monitoring or evaluation.

PRA is not only complemented by theatre, but theatre is also able to extend its possibilities. PRA uses techniques of diagramming for example, as a starting point for the analysis of community issues. These diagrams can be turned into improvisations discussing the possible outcomes of different solutions which can then be ranked or scored.[6] For example, Venn diagrams of institutional relationships can be brought to life by people acting out these relationships or creating silent images of them. Through the integration of words, movement and sound, participants are able to communicate their knowledge, opinions and thoughts. While PRA visualisation starts with what exists to focus discussions of what needs to change, the integration of theatre offers a means of visualising why and how changes might be necessary and might come about.

WHAT ARE THE DIFFERENT APPROACHES TO THEATRE AND DEVELOPMENT WORK?

It is useful to examine 2 contrasting approaches to Theatre and Development which provide the boundaries into which most practice falls. However, it is important to note that most practice rarely operates entirely within 1 approach.

Exogenous Theatre and Development

This approach is based on interventions and initiatives from outside the community or target group. Examples would be scripted didactic plays produced in order to promote a particular way of doing things. Exogenous Theatre is in some ways similar to 'banking education' discussed by Freire. The control of both the message and the medium remains with the outside expert and there is often little scope to offer spectators opportunities to explore their own realities.

Endogenous Theatre and Development

Endogenous Theatre and Development is rooted in the belief that change should be autonomous, from the inside out. The creation of performative or visual images is a starting point rather than a finished product and serves as a basis from which to begin to unravel and analyse the underlying issues and to work together to find solutions.

An illustration of how both endogenous and exogenous approaches may be present within one project can be found in the work of the Philippine Educational Theatre Association (PETA), which has employed theatre as a medium for more than 3 decades. Since 1967, it has been training young people through its summer workshops to become advocates of social reform. Using theatre, PETA has discussed issues such as urban squatting, demolition, tenant eviction, child prostitution, and child labour. PETA conducts theatre workshops as a process of social education. This process starts from a situational analysis and progresses to a point where participants identify possible alternative courses of action (endogenous development). These self-defined solutions are then presented to the other members of the community through pre-rehearsed presentations by local artists (exogenous development). PETA also rehearses and tours educational plays to local communities to pass on information about development issues (exogenous development).

One major example of endogenous Theatre and Development, on which many other approaches and projects are based, is Theatre of the Oppressed.

THEATRE OF THE OPPRESSED

Theatre of the Oppressed was developed in the early 1970s by Augusto Boal[7]. As a methodology, it is still evolving today through the continuing work of Boal, the Centre for the Theatre of the Oppressed based in Rio de Janeiro, Brazil and the many practitioners worldwide.

Theatre of the Oppressed is often advocated as a methodology or tool for participatory development as it offers a way for people to find their own solutions through analysis and action. The approach consists of an arsenal of popular theatre techniques including Image Theatre and Forum Theatre.[8] Forum Theatre uses rehearsed improvisations to create a scene of a specific oppression. It shows a person (the protagonist) who is trying to overcome an oppression but is hindered by people who place obstacles in his path (the antagonists). The scene is presented to an audience, and a *joker* (facilitator) invites the audience to intervene in the action, take the place of the protagonist and show them alternative ways to solve the problem.

Theatre of the Oppressed has many similarities to the pedagogical and political principles of Pedagogy of the Oppressed. Both pedagogies stress the need for thematic investigation carried out with the members of a community and the need to strive towards awareness of reality and self. Both also aim to demonstrate that alternatives exist to standard models of behaviour and ways of being in the world.

Theatre of the Oppressed is a participatory theatre that fosters democratic and co-operative forms of interaction to analyse and discuss problems of oppression and power and to explore group solutions to these problems. In Theatre of the Oppressed, *spectators* are replaced by *spect-actors* who have the opportunity to both act and observe and to analyse and dialogue with the events presented to them. Theatre becomes conscious intervention, a representation and rehearsal for real life and a collective analysis of common problems.

Boal extended the arsenal of Theatre of the Oppressed to include therapeutic theatre, which he presented in *The Rainbow of Desire*.[9] Boal developed this while in Europe in the 1980s when he realised that oppression had a different resonance for the Europeans with whom he was working. The oppressions were more likely to be internalised ones such as loneliness. These oppressions he termed 'The Cop in the Head'. He therefore worked with individual oppressions which could then be magnified to encompass a group or social reality:

> The notion of oppression thus expanded to include societal values – moral dictates pronounced by parents, peers, teachers, politicians, media, etc. – that obstruct our wills and foster passivity. Through TO [Theatre of the Oppressed] methods, these persistent and often disembodied voices are physicalised, animated, and addressed as 'real' antagonistic forces, in spite of their absence in the literal sense.[10]

Boal has also recently developed Legislative Theatre[11] which engages people in law making and social change through theatre. At the heart of the method are Forum Theatre and the spect-actor who intervenes in an unresolved scenario and attempts to break a cycle of oppression through a process which culminates in the creation of new laws.

HOW CAN THEATRE BE EMPLOYED TO MEET THE AIMS OF NGOS AND DEVELOPMENT AGENCIES?

Giving Voice
Using theatre-based techniques, the poor can tell their own stories, understand their own lives and confirm or challenge accepted ways of life and norms. Through theatre, participants can draw on their own life knowledge and life experience to create effective strategies and initiatives for change.

Creating Dialogue and Breaking Social Barriers
By telling their own stories, people increase their capacity for agency, become conscious actors in their own lives and thereby facilitate their own inclusion in development processes. Dialogue is facilitated between stakeholders and development professionals, others from within a community and all those who have traditionally shaped the stakeholders' lives.

Participation and Advocacy
The use of theatre-based techniques increases beneficiaries' confidence, self-awareness and self-worth, thus facilitating participation in aspects of community life such as access to the control and distribution of resources. People become advocates for their own needs and agents for change in their own lives.

Equality and Access
Promoting alternative methodologies also promotes the voices of those who are less often heard, particularly women and young people. Theatre supports the participation of new groups in development processes and facilitates this participation in new ways.

Creative Solutions
Theatre-based participatory development can facilitate a process whereby people reassess their initial assumptions and understanding of a situation. This in turn stimulates the exploration of alternative solutions, which can be rehearsed in the *safe space* of a workshop.

CONCLUSIONS
If participatory development is to facilitate change it must develop long-term strategies to challenge power inequalities at individual, organisational and community level. What is needed is a critical methodology that not only addresses inequities, but also strives to understand how those inequities arose and what maintains them. Empowerment can only occur when individuals, groups and communities are aware of the power relations in multiple aspects of their lives. Although social change begins with the individual who is first able to take action in her own life, it is vital for participatory practice to strike a balance between a focus on personal transformation and the development of a sense of agency, enabling the individual to take collective action to produce change at a wider scale.

Theatre-based participatory development can facilitate a process where people analyse and name their own realities and mobilise their individual and collective resources for change. Theatre can facilitate communication based on a horizontal rather than vertical plane which contributes to a realignment of power as the development expert, or facilitator, talks *with* rather than *at* a community.

END NOTES
1   Nyerere, J. (1973) *Freedom and Development*, Oxford University Press, Oxford.
2   Rowlands, J (1992) 'What is Empowerment?' in *Power and Participatory Development*, *Theory and Practice* (1995) edited by N Nelson & S Wright, Intermediate Technology, London.
3   *idem*
4   Freire, P (1972) *Pedagogy of the Oppressed*, Penguin, Harmondsworth

5   *idem*

6   See **Ex. 115 Mapping Your City** for an example of this.

7   Boal, A (1970) *Theatre of the Oppressed*, Pluto Press, London.

8   Boal, A (1992) *Games for Actors and Non-Actors*, Routledge, London.

9   Boal, A (1995) *The Rainbow of Desire*, Routledge, London.

10   Schutzman, M and Cohen-Cruz, J (1994) *Playing Boal*, Routledge, London.

11   Boal, A (1998) *Legislative Theatre*, Routledge, London.

AN EVALUATION OF THE USE OF THEATRE-BASED DEVELOPMENT TECHNIQUES IN NON-GOVERNMENTAL ORGANISATIONS IN RECIFE, BRAZIL

The Participatory Research Group was set up during the ARTPAD project to investigate the use of theatre-based participatory development techniques in the Northeast of Brazil. Over 5 months, participants from civil society organisations met twice a week for 3 hours to participate in workshops led by myself and Karla Galvao. The main objective of the group was to investigate the effectiveness of theatre in development projects, specifically in the work of the research group. In order to do this participants learnt and applied techniques, created new exercises and adapted existing material to meet their specific needs as facilitators.

Throughout this research process, the ARTPAD project co-ordinators and participants sought to answer a number of key questions:

- *Did participants make use of theatre techniques in their work as a result of their involvement in the project? If so, did the use of these techniques impact on the results that they achieved in their work outside the group?*
- *Did participation in the project impact on the way the facilitators worked with groups?*
- *How did participants evaluate the usefulness of theatre-based exercises in development projects in general?*

EVALUATION DESIGN

In order to answer these questions an evaluation process was planned which included:

- *A record of attendance*
- *Semi-structured interviews with all participants*
- *Three pilot studies of groups facilitated by participants*
- *Participant observation of workshops*
- *A creative evaluation session carried out in the last month of workshops*

The evaluation session was designed as an opportunity for participants to both evaluate the project and to try out some evaluation techniques which they could later apply in their own workshops. The following techniques were included:

1. Letters
Six pieces of card were placed on the floor, each with 1 letter on from the word A-R-T-P-A-D. Each piece of paper was divided into 2 columns – in 1 column there was a happy face and in the other a sad face. Participants were asked to write 2 words on each sheet of paper. The words had to start with the letter at the top of the page and express something positive or negative about the research process.

2. Matrix
Participants marked their responses to a number of questions about themselves and the project on a matrix using coloured stickers.

3. The Tree

We drew a large tree with roots, different types of branches, leaves and flowers. The tree had many different environments varying from barren ones to green rich areas. After explaining that the tree represented the professional life of each participant, we asked each person to stick a piece of paper (representing theatre) on the tree in the place that represented the relationship of theatre to their work. We asked participants to explain their choice of place on their piece of paper.

4. Venn Diagrams

Each participant designed a Venn diagram to illustrate the interaction of Theatre and Development with their professional and personal life. On the other side of the paper, participants were invited to write an explication of their diagram.

5. Photographs

Thirteen photos from different workshops were chosen as representing key moments from the workshops. Participants were asked to write comments under the photos, such as memories they provoked or issues that they raised.

6. Balloons

Each participant wrote a desire for the future (in relation to the project) on a piece of paper and put this piece of paper inside a balloon which they then inflated and stuck on the wall. At the end of the evaluation workshop, the participants threw the balloons in the air, burst them and then, in a circle, read out the anonymous messages they contained.

Participants had approximately 90 minutes to complete all the evaluation tasks in any order they chose. We endeavoured to provide a relaxed and informal atmosphere by providing music for the length of the workshop. Two participants commented that the room seemed like 'a big fun park'.

For the purpose of this evaluative study, I will focus on results from the creative evaluation workshop supported by evidence from the semi-structured interviews. The main questions addressed are:

- *What motivated participants to take part in the project?*
- *Did participants incorporate theatre-based techniques into their work?*
- *Did participation in the project impact on or change the way participants work?*
- *How useful did participants think theatre-based techniques were in participatory development work?*

GROUP PROFILE

The group originally consisted of 21 NGO facilitators from 18 civil society organisations. Although the majority of the participants were engaged in group work, they described their main responsibilities as follows:

> *Co-ordinators of organizations (5 participants)*
> *Facilitators (10)*
> *Psychologists (2)*
> *Social workers (1)*
> *NGO service users in the process of becoming facilitators (2)*
> *Teachers (1)*

Participants described the groups they worked with as consisting of:
> *Children (2)*
> *Adolescents / young people (16)*
> *Women (8)*
> *Men (6)*

ATTENDANCE

The workshops ran twice a week for 5 months but were interrupted by local elections, serious flooding and a police strike. The group initially had 21 participants but by December, this number had dropped to 17. Two of these 4 participants dropped out for personal reasons whilst the other 2 gave no reason.

Average attendance figures
August ------------------ 76%
September ------------ 77%
October ---------------- 81%
November ------------ 67%
December ------------- 58%

The majority of participants showed a high level of personal commitment to the project. Workshops were carried out in participants' own time, with the majority receiving no time off in lieu from work. Many participants found it difficult to arrive on time because of work commitments and pressures:

> I had to fight and say no, I have to get there, I have to be there and I think I was sometimes late ... sometimes I didn't even turn up because I couldn't manage it, my body just couldn't do it, it just wasn't possible.
> Roseane

Attendance dropped slightly in November and then further in December. At a group meeting, participants justified absences explaining that workload was particularly heavy in these months due to end of year evaluations, planning for the New Year, funding application deadlines and the end of the financial year. It was recommended that any future courses end in November.

WHAT MOTIVATED PARTICIPANTS TO TAKE PART IN THE PROJECT?

Fourteen members of the group already had some experience of using theatre in their work in civil society organisations. Experience varied greatly from the occasional use of improvised scenes to 'get a message across' to, in 3 cases, the facilitation of groups where social issues were discussed through theatre:

> I used it [theatre] quite a lot, with almost all my groups I tried to use theatre techniques ...
> And in this work with midwives, we specifically used theatre as a course methodology. Also during training, there were moments when the midwives did improvisations around the themes they were exploring.
> Ivete

Four of these 14 participants had received some formal training as art-educators and 3 had experience as actors or puppeteers. The remaining 7 participants had no experience of participating in or applying theatre-based techniques. In interviews carried out towards the end of the workshop period, the majority of participants recalled that they had expected theatre-based techniques learnt during the project to be of benefit to them in their work. Expectations of how useful the course would be had no correlation with participants' previous experience of theatre work:

> I am co-ordinating a project with adolescents, and the idea of learning more about exercises and theatre techniques to use with my groups motivated me a lot ... my greatest expectation was to discover, to get to know techniques which could be used to work on non-verbal language in a dynamic and captivating way.
> Lucia

One participant (a psychologist) had some knowledge of art therapy and, as she had recently started working in an NGO, was keen to see whether theatre could help her address some of the problems she encountered with group work:

I was interested in continuing work which I had already started by combining artistic work with social intervention. But previously, I had looked at this from a therapeutic standpoint and now the emphasis was on social intervention. I was interested to see if, together with the rest of my team in PAPAI, we would adapt the methodology we had been using with a certain group which hadn't been working very well.
Maristela

There was one dissenting voice. Janayna was very resistant to the idea of using games and theatre-based exercises in her work, but decided to participate in the group to see if her 'prejudice' was justified:

I wanted to beat this strong prejudice that I had against the use of group dynamic exercises, as I had had some quite unpleasant experiences in workshops which used them.
Janayna

EVALUATION MATRIX

During the creative evaluation session, participants were asked to respond to the following questions by placing their answer in one of four columns. A summary of the results is set out below.

	Strongly Agree	Agree	Disagree	Strongly Disagree	No Answer
I learnt about the techniques and the possibilities for their use	8	9	0	0	0
I can adapt the techniques to meet my own professional objectives	15	2	0	0	0
I am using theatre in issue-based work in my place of work	11	4	0	0	2
My professional practice has changed as a result of my participation in the project	12	5	0	0	0
The organisation I work for encourages the use of theatre in my practice	8	6	1	1	1

Summary of Findings

- *Of the 17 who participated in the above evaluation, 6 had no previous experience of working with theatre.*
- *All 17 participants stated that they had learnt about theatre-based techniques and the possibilities for their use in the development field and were able to adapt the techniques to their individual professional objectives.*
- *Of these 17, 15 stated that they were currently using theatre-based techniques   they had learnt through the project.*
- *All participants stated that their working practices had changed to some degree as a result of their participation in the project.*
- *Fourteen participants stated that they were encouraged to participate in the project by their work colleagues and supervisors.*

A more detailed analysis of these findings can be made by drawing on information provided by semi-structured interviews with each participant. These interviews were carried out in the final 2 months of the workshop process.

HAVE PARTICIPANTS INCORPORATED THEATRE-BASED TECHNIQUES INTO THEIR WORK?

Participants reported the introduction of theatre-based techniques in the following initiatives (organisations in brackets):

* *The gestation and evaluation of development projects (CENAP, Cais do Parto)*
* *Group work with HIV positive men and women (ASAS)*
* *Power dynamics within working groups and organisations (CENAP, ASAS, PAPAI, Mulher Maravilha, Outro Lado do Sol)*
* *Discussing women's history (SOS CORPO)*
* *Prevention of violence (PAPAI)*
* *Gender education (Mariama, PAPAI, Bemfam, Do Outro Lado do Sol)*
* *Prevention of HIV/AIDS (Bemfam, Gestos, Grupo Mulher Maravilha)*
* *Literacy training (Centre of Education – Federal University of Pernambuco)*
* *Discussing citizenship with adolescents (Centro Cultural Luis Freire, CDVCA, Ass. Moradores de Campo Grande, ASAS).*

The participants who already had experience of using theatre in their work before the project began, have now begun to use it in different ways. As a result, they have all found that workshops have a greater impact on participants. For example, Roseane from Mulher Maravilha explains:

> *The male adolescents started getting on better ... the boys didn't like to touch each other, to show each other any physical affection, because they are men and men don't do those things. This situation got a lot better. We had been doing some exercises of this type with the group, but we hadn't got very far with them ... after using theatre techniques, they started getting on with each other better. Everyone started to talk more, everyone got more involved and to like what they were doing. The boys have said that they like the workshops more now because they have changed and are a lot more fun and positive.*
> Roseane

The 6 participants who had no previous experience of using theatre-based techniques, all integrated techniques into their work during the project. Gilda for example, integrated techniques into workshop sessions in her organisation:

> *I didn't know anything about the idea of running a workshop using theatre-based techniques. In the workshops for counsellors, we worked a lot on the question of physical contact ... people with HIV need that contact because of the distance and apathy that are very common in the world. When a person with HIV comes looking for counselling, he [sic] is looking for someone who is able to touch him, who can squeeze his hand, can give him that hug ... so we need to work on that amongst ourselves. Everyone in the group understood that very well ... the group evaluated the day as really being very valuable. We were given compliments by the co-ordinators, it was really good.*
> Gilda

Janayna adapted techniques for use in the language classroom:

> [I can] adapt the exercises to the needs of those learning literacy skills. For example,
> yesterday I used Ex. 72 **What Are You Doing?** with the group and I stressed the idea of the
> incongruity of what you say compared with what you do and it stimulated a really good
> discussion among them.
> Janayna

Many participants not only made use of techniques in group work, but also during training workshops within their own organisations and when offering training to other professionals, for example:

> I used the techniques a lot with my own team when I became co-coordinator of CENAP ... I
> have been planning my activities with the idea in mind of using Theatre and Development
> techniques. For example ... I have to organise a meeting with instructors and monitors of a
> 3-month course which CENAP ran, so I am planning to use some of these techniques and I
> want to use some of those activities we did in that evaluation workshop.
> Ivete

By the end of the workshop period, at least 3 participants had begun generating extra income through the use of new skills and knowledge and others told of plans to do the same. Janayna, for example, is a school teacher who has now begun working in other fields:

> In January we were able to pass on some of what we had learnt and it was marvellous.
> We worked for 2 weeks at Instituto Vida reviewing and reflecting on everything. I have also
> used the techniques in the Alfabetização Solidária [national literacy campaign] and in the
> training of volunteer teachers which was very productive and what is more, was a job I got
> paid for.
> Janayna

Other participants were planning new initiatives based on their experiences in the project:

> In two of them [projects] that I am going to start soon, the techniques are essential, theatre
> has a fundamental role, it is a principal element ... one of the projects I developed this year
> concerns STD / AIDS and older people, it is for established groups of older people ... it is
> financed by the Ministry of Health and is very interesting because among all the activities
> there is a theatre group that will visit various communities to talk about issues such as
> sexuality and the rights of older people, prevention of infection, solidarity, gender and
> citizenship, these themes will all be aired by the theatre group.
> Dayse

ASSIMILATION

The degree of assimilation of theatre-based techniques into participatory development work varied greatly from participant to participant, and was influenced by many factors including:

- *Opportunity given in organisations to try new methodologies*
- *Current work status (some participants were unemployed)*
- *Attitude of organisations to Theatre and Development*
- *Current activities of partner organisations.*

A number of participants used techniques from the workshops at every group work session. One person reported that the 'worksheets are always in my hands ... I take them home sometimes because I'm always looking for a technique I can use'. Another described how the group she worked with would ask her for a new technique every week and would then take these techniques and use them in other contexts:

> They talked about the growth of the work and talked about the exercises, they talked about the importance of the games, of how they played them at school, at home, amongst themselves before I arrive. So you see the dimension this has taken on in their lives and what this can facilitate.
> Enidja

A small number of participants only used the techniques for warm ups or for closing a session. Two participants have not had an opportunity to use many of the techniques, as they were not currently engaged in group work.

DID PARTICIPATION IN THE PROJECT IMPACT ON OR CHANGE THE WAY THAT PARTICIPANTS WORK?

Participants were asked to describe any impact their participation in the project had on the way they worked with groups. The majority of participants described changes in the way their groups were functioning. The main changes observed were:

- Better integration of group members
- Clearer expression of thoughts and feelings
- Less reluctance to 'open up' by participants
- Less reliance on the spoken word and on sit-down discussions by participants
- Increased participation by group members
- Improved attendance at workshops.

Katia and Suzany summarise their experiences:

> They are able to express themselves more, they really are, and in this group we have noticed that even when we are sitting talking with them, that there is a new maturity in the way they speak. I think it's because of these exercises which stimulate a process. When one uses these techniques I think things flow better and the group develops, even in the way they speak.
> Katia

> There has been a very marked growth in the group ... they are more open with each other ... we have noticed new unity and the development of the concept of confidentiality – of not talking about things that happen in the workshop outside of the group, because it is only relevant to the people in the group. They have therefore begun to open up, to show their feelings and it has been easier to work with them this way.
> Suzany

Participants were asked to observe any general changes in the way that they worked as facilitators or as staff members of an organisation. Although all 17 participants believed that their practice had changed as a result of their participation in the project, 2 people commented that the project had simply served to reinforce practice they were already carrying out. More than half the remaining participants noted that their participation had resulted in greater confidence in taking that role and an increased openness to experimenting with new techniques and ideas:

I think I have become a little more relaxed as a facilitator as these exercises make you feel more comfortable ... and you have more ways of being innovative and of doing something different when you need to.
Maristela

Eight participants observed that their participation in the project had led them to consider important general issues regarding workshops and facilitation. These issues included:

- Safety of group members
- Respecting the limits of the group

I also learnt that we have to remember to take care, to observe people's limits, to see if they really want to participate, if they are really at a stage where they can, to set physical boundaries ... I have been looking at the idea of physical boundaries, of the limits of each individual. I didn't worry about this before, but now I see people more active, more participative and more interested [in my workshops].
Gilda

- Structuring a workshop
- The importance of planning

When I used exercises, they were one offs, for example, I didn't plan a theme for a workshop, sometimes I worked on various things simultaneously and they were sometimes a bit confused. This can be interesting because it invigorates the group, but perhaps it doesn't bring the same results, no it certainly doesn't bring the same results as a planned workshop.
Suzany

At least 4 participants noted that they now relied less on the spoken word in workshops and that this had brought benefits to both themselves and to their participant groups:

I think that the big difference is the priority given to body language. Often, verbal language is not that necessary – this has been a great lesson for me ... the exercises often speak without the need for words – they let the body speak.
Lucia

CONCLUSION

The research process was designed to discover how useful participants found theatre-based techniques in their work and whether their participation in the project had changed their ideas about theatre as a tool for participatory development.

Fourteen participants changed their ideas about the possible use of theatre in their work. Typical of the comments made is the following excerpt from an interview with Natan:

When I used theatre, when I did theatre, I concentrated on creating a show that [the public] would be satisfied with, I was worried about producing a show which was good and which the public would like. I didn't think about the kind of show that makes people ask questions about certain things. Today I have another vision of what theatre can do ... even if the audience don't like it so much, it can raise questions and issues.
Natan

Participants evaluated the usefulness of theatre in the following ways:

- Theatre facilitates participation
- Theatre involves both the participants and the public in the development process

You're there talking about drugs and they're there interacting with theatre and this is really great because it engages people more, people begin to speak, to move, to express themselves in a way that's really great, really communicative.
Roscane

As soon as I use it [theatre] I notice that people are more receptive … communication with them improves, it has an immediate effect.
Janayna

- Theatre acts as a catalyst for action:

The power that the techniques have is to make things happen. I have worked with a variety of methodologies over time, but when I use these techniques I am always surprised in some way.
Maristela

- Theatre helps you talk about your own life:

In one workshop I facilitated, the young people involved felt really safe in the work they were doing … they talked about a lot of personal issues, were very sincere about their own lives … they [the techniques] weren't only masks or games.
Janayna

- Theatre stimulates spontaneity and allows serious issues to be addressed through play:

I have looked for other ways to facilitate communication, spontaneity, the expression of feelings – this has been one of my main objectives. I think that through this experience, my range has been broadened, principally with more spontaneous and dynamic ways of working. For example, do you know what they say? It's like this: "are we going to play today?" For them it is a way of talking seriously through play, or of feeling something through a game.
Lucia

THREE CASE STUDIES

The aim of these case studies is to research ways that theatre is used in development projects and to create and test new techniques. Many of the participants had some previous experience of working with role play and games for building group co-operation, but most had never considered the idea of working on issues such as sexuality or citizenship through theatre. The workshops were, therefore, a catalyst for the inclusion of theatre-based participatory techniques into the methodology of the majority of participants in the studies.

The case studies followed 3 facilitators as they incorporated these techniques into their work with: a group of young men co-ordinated by Programa PAPAI (accompanied for 4 months), a weekly group with young women from Majê Molê dance group (accompanied for 4 months) and literacy trainers at NUPEP, Federal University of Pernambuco (accompanied for 3 sessions). A qualitative research study was designed for each group based on participant observation, semi-structured interviews, theatre-based research techniques, field diaries and some participatory evaluation techniques such as **Ex. 132 Graffiti Wall** and **Ex. 134 Photos**. The **Graffiti Wall** for example, was permanently available to workshop participants and created a space where participants could express themselves through images and words.

The following are case studies of these 3 experiences.

CASE STUDY 1

THE YOUNG MEN'S GROUP AT PROGRAMA PAPAI
co-authored with Karla Galvão, Maristela Moraes, Daniel Lima and Maria Adrião

PAPAI is a Brazilian not-for-profit civil society organisation based in Recife. This organisation works with men of varying ages in the Northeast of Brazil and conducts research, training and capacity-building in the fields of sexuality and reproductive health. PAPAI works at a local and international level in partnership with the Federal University of Pernambuco, principally in the areas of paternity in adolescence, the prevention of STDs and AIDS, gender-related violence, communication and health and drug use. Work with local people is divided into 3 interrelated areas: direct social intervention (weekly meetings with the target population in the form of group discussions, workshops and / or home visits), planning and evaluation meetings and workshops dealing with theory and methodology. One of the target communities is the Novaes Filho State School, situated in Várzea. This is an area with a largely low-income population, which is classified as highly vulnerable by the Municipal Secretary of Health.

The Novaes Filho School is one of the largest in the region, serving a student population of 1600 from Várzea and the surrounding area. PAPAI works at the school with a group of young men between the ages of 15 and 21, with the aim of addressing issues of gender and violence through youth action and participation.

This case study discusses the introduction of theatre-based techniques to the young men's group and the benefits that such a methodology has brought.

At the beginning of 2000, various attempts were made to establish and maintain a young men's group to discuss issues related to gender, sexuality and violence. Initially, it was not easy to guarantee the continuing participation of the young men in the group as, with the exception of 1 participant (a member of a religious youth group) none of the young men had ever engaged in any issue-based work. At the group's first meeting, the young men appeared en masse, curious to know what was going to happen in the group, but as their curiosity was satisfied, attendance levels gradually fell. During this period, the team from PAPAI identified the many difficulties inherent in group work with men, where it is necessary to create a continuing demand for sessions from a population which is generally socialised into not sharing their experiences with others. The challenge for the PAPAI team was therefore to create a legitimate work space which the participants identified and celebrated as being theirs. To achieve this, the facilitators and the group would need to work to create a space for listening and development with and for the young men.

At this time, the methodology chosen by the team became crucial to the success of the group. The PAPAI team began to question the methodology they had been using and to evaluate whether or not they had successfully facilitated the integration of the group, which needs had not been met and how these could be addressed with a new approach.

Thus far, workshops had been based around activities such as collages, educative videos, posters, music and group discussions. The facilitators now decided to introduce theatre-based techniques that they had learnt through their participation in the ARTPAD Project.

Initially, the facilitators imagined that theatre-based exercises would be rejected by a group of young, urban working-class men for whom theatre and physical expression were firmly identified as outside of the models of masculinity available to them. However, the team was surprised by the results:

> In the first group where we introduced these techniques, I said, "this could be really difficult, I don't know if it's going to work". It was a new way of working with sound and the body. It was completely different from what they [the young men] had been working on in the previous workshops. So, I think it was a great surprise for us and gave us great satisfaction too.
> PAPAI Facilitator

From this moment on, the workshops changed and there was an increase not only in attendance, but also in the frequency of the workshops:

> They [the young men] were really different. They were much more relaxed and participated a lot more … we realised that we had found the direction we needed to follow. The other sessions were a continuation of what we had created – the expectation from this first session … I had never seen the boys leave so happy from a workshop … they left the room jumping up and down, making the sounds of every machine [the closing exercise of the workshop], up to the school gate.
> PAPAI Facilitator

The facilitators began to use theatre-based exercises to deal with specific issues including gender, father–son relationships, drug use and gender-related violence. Through the use of theatre-based techniques, a new richness and depth emerged in the group's treatment of these issues. For example, in one workshop, the facilitator asked the group to construct a mural using their own bodies, which would tell the story of Pedro (a fictitious character). When the group read the story of Pedro from the mural, they introduced various elements from their own lives into the story including strong indications of violence, which had not been previously revealed:

> At a given moment ... Pedro received a death threat and he joined a church. One of the parts of the mural was a boy with a bible under his arm coming out of a church. After the exercise we asked about this incident, whether it was something that happened often, if they knew anyone who had been through that. We had no idea … they told us that it was very common, it was one of the most common ways to escape, you either die or you become an evangelical Christian to escape from that situation.
> PAPAI Facilitator

Both the facilitators and the group members were therefore able to gain a much better understanding of the life of each participant:

> *They weren't just doing theatre, they were expressing themselves, without any difficulty.*
> *They spoke of their own lives, contextualising their problems and even more importantly,*
> *discussing them without masks, without hiding, without fear and with sincerity.*
> PAPAI Facilitator

Fathers and Sons

Subsequently, group members gradually began to define the themes they wanted to work on for themselves. One such theme was father–son relationships. During this workshop, the facilitator used a Theatre of the Oppressed technique, **Ex. 112 Image of the Word**. Once more, the dimension of violence present in the daily lives of the participants was made evident. Images of authoritarian fathers and submissive sons, of violent men, alcoholics, scenes of humiliation, men hitting their sons and wives were created and discussed.

Finally, after the large number of negative images had been created, the group was asked to create images of an ideal father–son relationship. The resulting images were of a father embracing his son, a warm handshake between father and son and various other images where fathers and sons expressed mutual affection. Through these images, the team observed the immense capacity that participants had to reflect on and reconstruct this relationship in a positive way.

Real Men Don't Do Theatre

During this period of work, the team constantly evaluated the process by employing a number of theatre-based evaluation exercises. In one workshop, for example, participants were asked to work in pairs and to mould each other into images of the word 'theatre'.

The young men went on to mould stereotypical images of homosexuals, refusing to discuss or to interpret the images of the other participants – and did not recognise or acknowledge that they were using theatre to communicate. They had found a language which had given them a voice, but in name, this language was foreign to them and to be rejected because of its cultural associations. The group emphasised that they weren't doing theatre and that 'theatre isn't a thing for a man'.

What therefore, asked the facilitator, is a proper activity for a man? Over the next few sessions, the facilitator was able to work on an understanding of gender and masculinity with the group, constantly referring back to the understanding the group had constructed of the word 'theatre' – a theme apparently distant from the issues of human rights, citizenship or gender equality.

Conclusion

The young men from Novaes Filho began to appropriate theatre-based techniques as a way of communicating with the world after demonstrating very strong resistance to the idea of doing theatre. By adapting her workshop plans, the principal facilitator was able to negotiate this resistance and work alongside the group to investigate the rich material that the workshops produced:

> *Using theatre, I was surprised with the contents that appeared. It was all very rich, very vital.*
> *It was really good to feel that this resource let us work in safety, allowing us to touch on*
> *themes that seemed delicate or difficult, without shame, fear or frustration.*
> PAPAI Facilitator

MAJÊ MOLÊ AT THE NASCEDOURO IN PEIXINHOS

Majê Molê is an Afro-Brazilian dance group working with adolescent girls and young women in the Peixinhos neighbourhood of Olinda, Brazil. The group is co-ordinated by a community worker and a professional dancer and has been in existence for 3 years. At the time of this study, Majê Molê had 18 members between the ages of 13 and 24 who guarantee their places in the group by maintaining good school grades and attendance records.

The group is funded through a combination of private donations and fees for their frequent public performances. The girls do not receive personal fees when they dance as all income is directed towards covering essential running costs such as travel, food and costumes. The girls' relationship with the group is not therefore based on financial reward, but on affection, self-esteem, the value the group is given in the local community and a passion for dance. The group also provides a unique opportunity to dance at a professional level.

Psychology and Dance

In 2000, Majê Molê co-ordinators decided that for the group to continue to develop and work together, participants would need to address both social issues, such as citizenship, and personal issues within the group including conflict between participants. Enidja, a psychologist from the local NGO Mariama, was therefore brought in and she immediately began individual psychotherapy sessions with the dancers. Some months later, Enidja also began a *grupo informativo* (informative group) with the girls. This session lasted for one and a half hours every week and was designed to provide a space for the girls to examine issues collectively. It was into these sessions that Enidja decided to incorporate theatre-based techniques.

Peixinhos and Majê Molê

The dancers from Majê Molê live in the community of Peixinhos; an urban area which manifests the numerous social problems common to poor city neighbourhoods including extreme poverty, inadequate provisions for health and education and a high crime rate. However, what differentiates Peixinhos from other neighbourhoods in the area are its very active cultural movements which play a major role in the positive image that surrounding communities have of Peixinhos. Two local buildings are also important to the area in this respect; the market, which serves the large local population and the old abattoir which has been transformed into a cultural centre known as the Nascedouro (a play on the word birthplace), where local groups, including Majê Molê meet and rehearse.

Peixinhos is an area of socio-economic contrast, where the very poor live side by side with the middle classes. The percentage of inhabitants living below the poverty line is high and the area is known locally as a favela (an unofficial housing area lacking basic services). There is a high incidence of violence in the area, the victims of which are most commonly women and children. Additionally, abandonment (of children and spouses), neglect, sexual assault and the exploitation of children in drug trafficking are real and everyday problems, causing many inhabitants to feel vulnerable in and around their own homes.

A superficial analysis of power relationships in Peixinhos reveals a social structure based on hierarchies of class, ethnicity, gender and perceived worth. It is therefore possible to surmise and to demonstrate that the young, black, female participants of Majê Molê face inequality, prejudice and conflict on a daily basis. Some of these inequalities and prejudices have also been reproduced between the participants of the group, causing disputes regarding individual roles and status. The dancers' levels of self-esteem have also been seriously prejudiced by their identity as young, black females from a low-income community and by the disequilibria in gender relations and consequent physical and mental hardship.

Involvement in an Afro-Brazilian dance group has gradually increased the girls' status in the local community as they have begun to travel outside of Peixinhos, dance in public, meet new people and appear in the local media. Although the girls are excluded from many aspects and areas of Brazilian life, it is possible to chart how, on becoming members of the dance group, a process of acceptance and integration has begun. This process is limited by clearly defined boundaries of space (the process advances when the girls are on stage) and time (it ends when the girls return to the periphery – Peixinhos). As a result of this process, the status of the girls has increased as they are increasingly identified as 'famous young women' rather than as poor, teenage girls, and are therefore valued as objects of pride and envy in a society which generally rarefies women's bodies and experiences.

The group's excursions to the world outside of Peixinhos have additional significance in the community as many residents of Peixinhos have never even travelled to other areas of Greater Recife because of their limited financial resources. These trips have also widened the girls' perspectives and expectations and have allowed the girls to gain a glimpse of another life – of what life could be – away from an area characterised by the problems of drug trafficking, prostitution and drug addiction, all of which have had either a direct or indirect impact on the lives of the girls.

The value conferred on Majê Molê by local residents, the media and the general public has been of huge benefit to the girls, but has conversely also been the cause of tension and conflict between individuals in the group. When Enidja began working with Majê Molê, she observed that conflict had been polarised by the attention and praise that the girls received and that they had formed clearly identifiable sub-groups generated by, and in turn generating, power struggles and prejudice.

The Introduction of Theatre-based Techniques
Enidja decided to introduce theatre-based techniques into the group workshops as a way of addressing social and personal issues that had arisen during individual sessions and group rehearsals. A number of specific issues were selected by the facilitator including sexuality and citizenship and it was hoped that the use of theatre would give a voice to the girls and allow them to raise and discuss the problems most pertinent to them. One issue which the girls brought to the sessions was the way in which their neighbourhood was viewed by both themselves and also by people that they met when performing in other parts of the city. The members of Majê Molê view their neighbourhood through the eyes of those who have returned from the outside and are therefore acutely aware of the problems that surround them. The girls were able to discuss their observations and the impact that certain realisations had on them through the use of techniques such as **Ex. 114 Mapping my Neighbourhood** and **Ex. 115 Mapping your City**. During these sessions, the girls also expressed the significance that the group had in their lives. When, for example, they were asked to map the route they took from home to the Nascedouro building, without exception they all used the houses of other group members as their principle references, demonstrating an important personal network. During **Mapping Your City**, the girls expressed a desire for their neighbourhood not to be known solely as a favela and talked about various aspects of life in Peixinhos. They particularly stressed the importance of the cultural movement and the many positive changes that had occurred in their day-to-day lives since they had become members of the dance group.

As the workshops progressed, the girls began to use the theatre-based techniques to speak about their own lives in a way which Enidja identified as 'more self-possessed and less self-conscious'. For example, one of the many interpersonal difficulties displayed by the group was the power held by the older girls, who had formed their own sub-group, over the younger ones. During **Ex. 119 The Mural Inca**, which the group was using to discuss the history of Majê Molê, the girls divided into 2 groups (the younger girls on one side of the room and the older girls on the other). As they began to tell the Majê Molê story through frozen images, the participants slowly began to integrate into 1 group and deconstruct the unequal power relationship between them. The process of joint story telling acknowledged the existence of a shared history, whilst the success of the exercise confirmed the ability of the group to create something with 1 voice. After this exercise, the younger girls began to express their feelings and opinions more freely and their participation in the workshops increased.

When asked to describe changes that had taken part in the group during the workshops, some of the girls related:

> We changed the way we were acting, the way we spoke and we started talking about our problems and feelings and we were able to talk about our emotions.

> [With these exercises] we got to a point where we were able to accept what each other said and things got a lot better.

> I have noticed that I used to be very quiet and that now I am more relaxed about speaking to the others. When teachers used to ask my opinion I didn't speak, but now I do.

During subsequent workshops, other theatre-based exercises were introduced to the group such as **Ex. 16 The Mad Chicken**, **Ex. 4 My Name in Action**, **Ex. 108 The Machine**, **Ex. 74 Grandma's Footsteps**, **Ex. 41 Pass the Pulse** and **Ex. 112 Image of the Word**. When interviewed, the girls described how these exercises had helped them to express themselves, to talk about their own lives and to examine how they felt about themselves. One of the girls described how **My Name in Action** had helped her to share her dreams with the group. She related how she had associated her name with the profession of journalist and that this had been important as she had been able to re-present herself to the group by describing her dreams for the future rather than her physical appearance or other characteristics of which the rest of the group were already aware. The exercise was a way to tell the others something new about herself. Other girls also highlighted the importance of the workshops in helping them to express their desires and also to talk about their day-to-day lives. For example:

> I talked about sadness and stress. When we do a show, a lot of the girls get nervous ... and we always end up either all stressed out or really happy.

> The other workshops are for dancing or other things, but not this one ... it's about something you have to let out from deep inside yourself.

A number of other exercises were used by the facilitator specifically to improve inter-personal relationships in the group. **Ex. 133 The Present**, for example, was used at the end of a workshop as a way of evaluating and closing the session. Through the giving of imaginary presents, which included an apology and a thank you, the girls were able to communicate their feelings for each other:

> I was surprised because the girls weren't really talking to each other and during the exercise they relaxed, some of them cried. They talked about the difficulties that had led to them falling out with each other, they made peace with each other. And from that point on, the situation got easier; there was more communication and a better understanding of the events that had led to this situation.
> Enidja – Facilitator

Through the use of theatre-based exercises, the sessions became a space in which group conflicts could be expressed and resolved. For example, group members were able to analyse and discuss the division of tasks between participants and to talk about relationships both within and outside the group. Within Majê Molê, relationships between the girls became easier whilst externally an awareness of rights and what they meant to each individual girl gave them a new structure through which to view their world, based on an understanding of how issues of gender and citizenship impacted on their lives. A change also took place in the subject matter that the group was willing to deal with, as participants introduced new issues and also revealed new personal information, demonstrating themselves willing to discuss these with both the group and the facilitator. For instance, whilst using images theatre to discuss the issue of sexuality, the girls created images that specifically showed their personal understanding of the theme and permitted the facilitator to redirect the workshop and subsequently address their individual doubts and questions. Through a planned series of games, the girls worked with the facilitator and set their own agenda, bringing their own experiences to the group and allowing the fun aspect of the workshop to dissipate any embarrassment regarding the subject matter of the workshop:

> [In the group] we play a lot, we talk about the group, we listen to the opinion of everyone about STDs, we talk about sex, about equal rights, about unity and about having respect.
> Group member

Summary

Many changes were facilitated in the group through the use of theatre-based techniques. The exercises helped the girls to construct their own ideas around social issues and to begin to transform internal group conflict into mutual respect and understanding. Theatre also helped both the facilitator and the girls to identify the group's agenda to give a new clarity and purpose to workshops, as they increasingly became about the girls' problems, dilemmas and hopes:

> [Theatre] has been the instrument that has permitted each of the girls to see how much they can do … they may be just games, but these games revealed a lot to the girls about their lives. They are something concrete they can refer to when they talk to their mothers, their sisters, their father, teachers and say "no, no, I don't agree, I see things this way – I can see your point, but that's not the way I want to do things". Through play, the girls have strengthened their position as subjects in the social sphere – and that was my main objective – to recover that subject that was crumpled, worn down, discriminated against, disempowered, without any rights to express herself.
> Enidja – Facilitator

To be a young, black woman in a marginalised neighbourhood presents many challenges, not least when constructing self-esteem and inter-personal relationships and these difficulties have been eloquently expressed by the group through theatre-based exercises. The opportunity to examine their daily lives, to strive for greater self-esteem and to rethink their personal relationships within and outside Majê Molê has strengthened the girls in terms of their identity as individuals, as a group and as part of the Afro-Brazilian cultural movement.

CASE STUDY 3

WORKING WITH YOUNG PEOPLE AND ADULTS IN POPULAR EDUCATION
co-authored with Janayna Cavalcante (Universidade Federal de Pernambuco)

Context
The idea of integrating Theatre and Development workshops into the Youth and Adult Education (EJA) Training Programme emerged from a wish to broaden the methodological perspectives of EJA. It also came from a personal desire as a facilitator to investigate how theatre-based techniques could be integrated into a methodology for the re-socialisation[1] of young people and adults who have been socially excluded from basic education.

The concept of re-socialisation is the driving force behind the popular educational and literacy work of the Nucleus for Teaching, Research and Extension in Education of Young People and Adults (NUPEP), at the Centre of Education, Federal University of Pernambuco (UFPE), Northeast Brazil. Re-socialisation is a wide concept which delineates a process of transformation in the relationship of the individual to the world. These transformations are circumscribed by 2 other processes: recognition and reinvention. Recognition characterises the processes by which individuals restructure their vision and understanding of the world; reinvention represents, 'the work of the active mind; it is an act of understanding in which we reinvent our discourse through practice.'[2]

Through my participation in the workshops in Recife, I had come to the conclusion that theatre was a fundamental tool in the facilitation of processes where people speak, make themselves heard and empower themselves in decision-making processes. I had also concluded that theatre could facilitate work in popular education and bring new dimensions to issues that are generally marginalised in the educational curriculum such as gender, power relations, social development and reproductive health. The notion that theatre could be used to facilitate empowerment and give voice led me to surmise that theatre could also be integrated into the EJA approach of re-socialisation.

I therefore planned 3 workshops with literacy trainers at EJA, incorporating techniques I had learnt in training workshops. The general theme chosen for the workshops was 'Other Languages: creativity in the classroom'. The workshops would discuss the use of theatre-based exercises, an approach which was new to participants and could be used to transform the classroom into a space which was more pleasant and conducive to learning. To this end, our general aim was to examine 'the importance of creative strategies in the stimulation of communication and problem solving'. I also defined a number of objectives which I hoped to meet in the 3 sessions available to us:

1. *To integrate the group and discuss the need for and use of ice-breakers.*
2. *To discuss theatre as an important tool for community workers, specifically in the context of EJA.*
3. *To introduce the group to theatre-based techniques.*
4. *To discuss the importance of creativity in educational work.*
5. *To examine the work-related problems of individual group members.*
6. *To stimulate the participants to investigate and use new ways of working.*

The Group

The group was made of 25 municipal co-ordinators and trainers from the Federal Literacy Programme. All 25 participants were based in small or medium-sized towns in the interior of Brazil. The towns are in poor municipalities where one of the major indicators of a lack of social development is the high index of illiteracy among inhabitants. The national literacy programme receives funding from both public and private bodies and is designed to meet the needs of such towns. Pedagogical aspects of the programme are managed by Federal Universities including UFPE.

The main aim of the literacy programme is to reduce illiteracy levels nationwide and to therefore qualify the country to be internationally classified as 'in development'. The programme teaches basic literacy skills over a 5-month course and strives to make participants aware of the importance of the written words in their lives. After 5 months, it is hoped that participants will go onto further training in the formal education system.

The programme co-ordinators and trainers who were participating in the NUPEP workshops were between 22 and 35 years of age and were employed on this and other educational initiatives in their municipalities. The workshops formed part of an obligatory training course for all trainers and the theatre module was envisaged as a platform for the discussion of issues relevant to the performance and running of the entire programme.

The Facilitator

My challenge was to fit the needs and specificities of that group to a set of theatre techniques. I had to take into account that the group had already been working together for 10 days, far from home in a programme which they found very demanding. I started, therefore, from the supposition that the workshops should primarily be fun.

The First Workshop

After using the technique **Ex. 1 Kites and Balloons**, various questions relating to the training programme were brought up by the group. Despite making it explicit that the group should concentrate on questions relating specifically to the workshop in progress, many group members raised issues regarding the training programme as a whole. As we were in the middle of a discussion about the exercise, the general co-ordinator of the training programme came into the room and asked for a moment to speak with the group. The co-ordinator was about to leave on business and although the meeting had not been planned, it could not be scheduled for another time. The subsequent discussion was very productive as the problems were literally on the table, or better said, on the floor written on balloons and kites that the participants had produced. As the ultimate holder of authority in EJA, the co-ordinator was the very person that the group needed to speak to and he had appeared at the exact moment that the issues had been raised. This incident demonstrated how the use of different practice could open channels of dialogue where these channels had previously been blocked or made difficult. The process of speaking out, of expressing oneself, confronting others in public debate was facilitated by the exercise.

I verified my impressions through interviews and reports collected from the group during and after the workshops. The emphasis on words such as relaxation, calmness, feeling good and happiness, together with the association that the theatre-based techniques made their work more interesting denote the value the participants gave to the experience.

After the coffee break on the first day, I used **Ex. 16 The Mad Chicken** to warm up the group. I was wary of this exercise as I thought that the group might find it childish. This fear proved to be one that the group did not share. In fact, the technique revealed to me a group that, despite their fame for being argumentative and prone to complaining, were open to new activities and ideas – qualities essential in trainers. **The Mad Chicken, Ex. 35 Bombs and Shields**, **Ex. 121 Childhood Dreams** and other techniques that reawaken the playful side of people and their relationships facilitated excellent discussions of the day's themes. An example is the discussion which arose concerning the values inherent in cartoons and how these impact on children in our society. During the discussion, the participants positioned themselves as trainers and primarily as mothers (the male group members took a back seat in this discussion). The group concluded that children's cultural experience needed to be improved, that morals and ethics should be explored through culture. Despite this assertion, the group affirmed that it felt helpless and defenceless when confronted with their children's schools, the place where their children explored and asserted their values without, in the main, adequate guidance or support.

The use of theatre-based exercises allowed the group to look at issues, formulate questions and examine problems with renewed enthusiasm and at their own pace. **Ex. 14 Fruit Salad**, for example, was used by the group to explore common problems. The participants were so interested in their commonalities and differences that they stopped the game after each question to discuss the issues that had been raised. Planned to last for 20 minutes, the game took 1 hour to complete.

A Space to Speak

Having access to a space in which one can speak freely is essential to effective human interaction, especially in the contexts of personal and community development. Theatre seems to awaken the drive to find a personal space for expression, whether through the spoken word or through the use of the body.

When an organisation or process is run hierarchically, space for personal expression can be limited and be constrained or controlled by authoritarianism. Theatre can facilitate the bringing into the open of grievances and the construction of situations where all individuals can express their opinions and have them heard and respected. In the case of the EJA workshops, the group demonstrated the desire to express their opinions regarding the training programme, and the workshops became the vehicle through which they evaluated the programme and communicated their findings.

The Second Workshop

The objective of the second workshop was to explore the idea that problems become simpler if we change the way we look at them. To this end, I used **Ex. 112 Image of the Word** to address the participants' professional dilemmas. Participants spoke of truancy and the extended absences of their students, the problems associated with running literacy programmes at grassroots level and the pressure of the demands being made on them from all sides.

In the second workshop, the group had already become very interested in this new methodology. Interviews record that the group evaluate these workshops as the 'most useful' in the week-long course as they were a place for complicity, where the group felt at ease to criticise the structure of the course and its organisation.

This process has limits; in this case, the process was confined to 3 workshops. This leads me to key questions: What are the limitations of theatre as an actor in real life? How far can theatre go?

The Third Workshop

In the third workshop we looked back at the whole week and evaluated the programme. We also used theatre-based exercises to evaluate the level of integration in the group. For example, during the playing of **Ex. 28 Careful! Here Comes the Shark**, participants were finding it very difficult to work as a group until one of them pointed out that they should 'stick together until the end in the game as they had managed to stick together in the course'. Henceforth in this workshop, the participants displayed unity and co-operation as they completed activities and exercises.

Summary

The use of theatre-based exercises in the EJA programme provided the group with a space and language with which to look critically at their work and the work of EJA. It provided the group with an opportunity to play, to make themselves heard and to learn new ways of working. The experience also produced more solid and confident relationships between myself and the participants to the extent that after 1 year, participants still recall in great detail the debates and exercises experienced over the 3 sessions. At the most recent training session, although there were no theatre workshops scheduled, the group approached the co-ordination team and asked for sessions to be included in the programme.

END NOTES

1   Souza, João Francisco de (1999), 'A Educação Escolar, Nosso Fazer Maior, Desafia Nosso Saber', NUPEP, Recife: Bagaço.

2   *idem.*

THE FIRST WORKSHOP

Marcelo Alexandro Silva (Grupo Alto Falante – Centro Cultural Luis Freire)

The Alto Falante group at the Centro Luis Freire in Olinda, Greater Recife is a group of young people who participate together in workshops and theatre projects. ARTPAD ran sessions with the group with the aim of offering training and of testing techniques with young people who already had some experience of theatre-based work.

This poem was written by Marcelo, one of the group members, as a response to a request for written comments on the first workshop. It has been included in this book as an example of a creative evaluative text written by a young person and as an illustration of the significance of the workshops in his life.

The First Workshop
Cloudy
The weather was
Lousy
An insignificant morning
Was on the cards
The day began
The afternoon came
And at last
Time passed.
I arrived at the place
Inconsolable
I was tired
In a whirl
Time went slowly
But I was there.
I met someone
Great
Simple and radical
I listened
It was the first workshop.
I understood what to do
I learnt something new
Experienced everything
I hoped
And wanted.
We played games
We came through
Positive forces
People united as a group.
Beginning and renewing
We existed before
What vigour
A constant group
That has strength
Courage
Transcending any
Barrier
We'll swim together
To find self-esteem
In this sea of shadows
We'll get through things
And will never fall apart.

AN EVALUATION OF THEATRE AND DEVELOPMENT WORKSHOPS IN PERU

During 2001, the ARTPAD project undertook a Theatre and Development training programme in Peru. This was planned as a test phase for material developed by the participatory research group in Recife.

The initial plan was to offer a 3-day training courses for NGO workers in Theatre and Development techniques and to return a month later to evaluate, with the participants, the effectiveness of these techniques.

As we planned this phase of the project, we realised that there was a great demand for the training course outside of our original destinations of Lima and Cusco. Various requests were sent via e-mail asking for courses in diverse areas of the country. It was therefore decided to extend the training plan to include 2 new locations: Iquitos, the largest city in the Amazon region and Cajamarca, an Andean mining town. The criteria for inscription was widened to include any not-for-profit organisation that was interested in integrating theatre-based techniques into their working practices.

Other modifications had to be made due to the unexpected second round of the national presidential elections. After our experiences with local elections in Brazil, we predicted that many NGOs would be involved in campaigning or monitoring election arrangements, so the beginning of the Peruvian phase of the project was put back by a month. The result of these changes was that we would now be working with more organisations and individuals over a shorter period.

IQUITOS
The first training course was carried out in Iquitos and organised by La Restinga, a small local NGO working with child street workers. La Restinga arranged for a group of individuals to attend the workshops. The participants came from organisations working with a diverse range of communities and issues:

- *Gay rights*
- *Adults and children with special needs*
- *Indigenous Indian culture*
- *Indigenous Amazonian women*
- *Bilingual teacher training programme*
- *Child street workers*
- *Barefoot doctors*
- *Street educators*
- *Primary health care*
- *Homeless adolescents*
- *HIV/Aids.*

Group Profile
- *None of the participants had received any previous theatre training.*
- *None of the participants had ever consistently used theatre-based techniques in their work.*
- *Expressed interests: integration of participants, general group work and sexual health work.*

CAJAMARCA
In Cajamarca, the NGO Fotosintesis co-ordinated the workshops and used their institutional data base to enrol 27 participants active in the following areas:

- *Rural development*
- *Human rights*
- *Rural credit programmes*
- *The National Institute of Culture*
- *Women's organisations*
- *Home workers support*
- *Disabled adults training programme*
- *People with learning difficulties*
- *Citizenship*
- *Political participation*
- *Peasant farmer support / credit programmes.*

Group Profile
- *Four participants were members of theatre groups and used theatre-based techniques in their work.*
- *Fifteen participants had never used theatre-based techniques in their work.*
- *Expressed interests: sexual health and the environment. Both these themes have become central to NGOs' work in the area as a result of the biggest gold mine in Latin America recently opening in the town.*

LIMA

As the capital of Peru, Lima is home to hundreds of civil society organisations. We co-ordinated a group of 18 development professionals to take part in the 3-day workshop. This group was perhaps the most culturally and professionally diverse and included professionals from the following areas:

- *Afro-Peruvian culture*
- *Environmental education*
- *Indigenous culture*
- *Job training for the socially excluded*
- *Women's rights*
- *Sexual health*
- *Reproductive rights*
- *Human rights*
- *Eco-tourism*
- *Responsible paternity.*

Included in this number were 4 participants from the Amazon town of Pucallpa working in the environmental and tourism sectors.

Group Profile
- *Two participants were professional theatre practitioners.*
- *Eight participants had never used theatre-based techniques in their work.*
- *Eight participants had some experience of using role play.*

CUSCO

The final training course was held in Cusco. The 24 participants came from urban and rural-based organisations working in diverse areas including:

- *Alcohol abuse*
- *Domestic violence*
- *Agricultural development*
- *The promotion of traditional medicine*

- *Primary health care*
- *Gender education*
- *Community leadership*
- *Alternative agriculture*
- *Training young people for employment.*

Group Profile
- *None of the participants had received any previous theatre training.*
- *Nine participants had consistently used theatre-based techniques in their work.*
- *Fifteen participants had experience of using role play in their work.*
- *Expressed interests: integration of participants, general group work, sexual health and gender.*

EVALUATION

During an evaluation workshop carried out one month after their participation in the training course we asked thirty-eight of the participants in Iquitos, Cajamarca and Lima to respond to the questions below. Answers were recorded by the placing of coloured stickers on a poster.

	Strongly Agree	Agree	Disagree	Strongly Disagree	No Answer
I am going to use these techniques in my work	74%	18.5%	5%	0%	2.5%
I think my professional practice will change as a result of my participation in the workshops	60.5%	24%	2.5%	2.5%	10.5%
I can adapt the techniques to my specific work needs	45.5%	42%	2.5%	5%	5%
The training has been relevant to my work	74%	21%	2.5%	0%	2.5%

Summary of Table
- *Over 90% of participants asked said they would use the techniques they had learnt in their work.*
- *87% agreed that the techniques could be specifically adapted by them to their specific work needs.*
- *84% of participants who responded thought that their professional practice would change as a result of their participation in the 3-day workshop.*
- *95% felt that the workshop had been relevant to their work.*

Considerations for the Interpretation of Survey Results

Although we can see that participants saw the training as extremely relevant and useful for their professional practice, a number of factors must be taken into consideration in order to provide the overall picture.

- *The evaluation material was collected within a month of the training workshop whilst the experience and the techniques themselves were very fresh in the participants' minds.*
- *The evaluation was carried out by the facilitators of the original workshop who had formed personal relationships with many of the participants.*
- *We were only able to question 38 out of the original 69 participants of the 3 training courses. Of those absent, 26 justified their absence citing professional commitments or health problems.*
- *The 4 participants in Lima who had travelled from Pucallpa were unable to travel to Lima for the evaluation session.*

Using feedback from the evaluation session and e-mails received from 25 participants, the above questionnaire can be examined in more depth:

Question 1: I am going to use these techniques in my work

In each city, we heard a number of examples of how participants had begun using theatre-based techniques in their work. In Lima for example, Teatro del Milenio has created a project to deal with issues of sexual health and reproductive rights with Afro-Peruvian young people through theatre, music and dance. One facilitator has begun to use image theatre work with female political prisoners. In Cusco, a group of facilitators has formed an organisation to carry out group work around the issue of the environment and is planning to use and adapt nearly every exercise from the manual. One of their first clients is a multi-national firm who requested workshops for all their staff on local environmental issues.

The impact of the training course is exemplified by the experience of SER (Rural Education Services) who organised a training workshop entitled: 'The Use of Theatre in the Analysis of the Current Political Situation' (June 2001). This workshop was aimed at women community leaders, women's groups and organisations and was used to pass on techniques learnt at the ARTPAD workshop. The objectives of the workshop were to:

1. Train women leaders in the use of theatre as an instrument for the analysis of the political situation.
2. Examine the possibilities and limits of theatre-based exercises in this sphere.

Feedback from the workshop suggests that the community leaders present were receptive to the use of theatre in their work. During an evaluation, participants were asked to respond to the following question: 'After your experience in this workshop, what do you consider the usefulness of theatre in an analysis of the political situation?' Participants raised a number of points:

Theatre can be used to talk about difficult or taboo subjects:

> *I think it lets you tackle issues that may be abstract, difficult or controversial in a simple way, which facilitates discussion and understanding.*

> *It helps us, as people often don't like to talk or read about our political situation, and theatre helps us to know, visualising the ways our government has manipulated us at their whim and how we have managed to escape from this.*

Theatre work is inclusive:

> *It would be useful for women from marginal neighbourhoods as many of them don't have any schooling and are not literate, but they have a lot of fight and drive.*

Theatre work promotes authentic communication between individuals and groups:

Theatre is more participatory, more interactive, and for me has much more of an impact. It's really an excellent way to achieve deep levels of communication and a way of finding out what each participant thinks about a certain issue.

It shows our fights, victories, experiences, our hopes, in a real and dynamic way.

Summary of Question 1
• *Almost all participants strongly agree that they will use these techniques in their work.*
• *The range of techniques presented in the workshop is relevant to a wide variety of different contexts.*
• *Theatre can facilitate communication and represent our lives in an in-depth and dynamic way.*

Question 2: I think my professional practice will change as a result of my participation in the workshops

Eighty-four per cent of participants predicted that their professional practice would change as a result of participating in the ARTPAD workshops. Many participants immediately incorporated exercises from the training into their working practice. Some achieved this in quite radical ways. For example, in a residential home for disabled children, the worker responsible for assessing and monitoring children's abilities found that the use of theatre-based techniques revealed otherwise hidden physical and mental skills.

Another participant related:

The manual was very useful to us, we used it with an institution called ELIC, that works with children with learning difficulties. They came to us because they [the facilitators] were very timid, couldn't talk about their experiences easily and were therefore having problems in workshops. I say "were", because after using nearly all the exercises for group integration and warming up, they are more awake, they come across much better and have more ideas for working with the children.
Facilitator, NGO Cedur Ununchis

Summary of Question 2
• *The evidence from this and other examples shows that the training has impacted on professional practice in the following areas:*
  • *Teaching styles*
  • *Teaching methods*
  • *Relationships between group leaders and participants*
  • *An increased understanding of the importance of group integration.*
  • *An increased ability to facilitate group integration.*

Questions 3 & 4: I can adapt the techniques to my specific work needs / The training has been relevant to my work

In Iquitos, La Restinga has used many of the integration exercises with child street workers who visit their centre (a house in the centre of Iquitos).

Over the last 3 weeks we have put into practice some of the techniques you taught us. I'm really pleased with the results, pleased and surprised. I had already put aside my prejudice against exercises and games, but until now, I hadn't put any of them into practice. We had a creative and informative day working on STDs and AIDS with 54 adolescents and children. In 5 groups they worked for 20 minutes on exercises and games for ice breaking, trust and

warming up, we taught some of the other facilitators some techniques which worked really well. Then the groups went round a circuit of 5 exercises about sexuality and prevention, and then every group presented a sketch to the others.
Luis Gonzales-Polar, La Restinga

Many organisations have sent me adaptations they have made to techniques for their own purposes. One example is **Ex. 116 1001 Uses for a Condom**. I suggested this exercise for use in workshops on sexual health, especially with young people. One organisation in Peru has adapted it to discuss the environment, more specifically the disposal of solid waste matter:

We managed to adapt various techniques, for example, for the management of solid waste, we gave the group material that could be recycled (tins, plastic bottles, paper etc.) and then asked them for suggestions on how they could be re-used … in this way we were able to make the group aware.
NGO Worker, Cusco, Peru

Many participants have developed training programmmes into which they integrated theatre-based techniques. These include programmes on human rights, sexual health, sustainable development and eco-tourism. One such course was carried out by Bertha Munoz at Processo Social in Lima. She designed and executed the workshop: 'Theatre techniques for participation in the education of girls, boys and adolescents: a workshop on the rights of the child' (June 2001) with public sector school teachers. The workshop was originally based upon discussion and pen and paper learning. Below you will find the plan for her workshop:

Theatre techniques for participation in the education of girls, boys and adolescents: a workshop on the rights of the child

Day 1
Objectives: Integrate the group
What rights do children have?
Sensitise the group to the issue

Warm up	My Name in Action
Introducing the theme	Brain Storm
	Image of the Word – in small groups, participants make images of the different rights that children have
	Pilot/co-pilot to discuss personal stories of childhood related to theme, so participants relate their own lives to the theme
Energy release	The Mad Chicken (release energy / emotion after the intensity of the previous exercise)
Integration	Cat and Mouse – to prepare for more work on the issue
Issue work	Bully, Victim, Saviour – to discuss social roles in the protection and assertion of rights
Question and answer session	Balloons Participants write messages or doubts about the rights of the child inside balloons. In a circle the group discuss these anonymous comments

Day 2
Objectives: Investigating techniques for education work on rights with boys, girls and adolescents

Integration	Mirrors (negotiation, leadership, power)
	Things in Common
Issue work	Looking at children's games to discuss how these are influential in issues of equality and rights
Warm up	How Many Ways to Say Hello
	Fruit Salad
Theme	Chairs – discuss issues of co-operation, power, negotiation
Issue work	TV News – raise issues relating to rights, find out how much the group know
Evaluation	Papier-mâché – to evaluate the workshop

Summary of Questions 3 & 4
- Participants felt encouraged and motivated to try new methods and approaches in their work.
- Some workers were surprised at how receptive different communities were to theatre-based work.
- The techniques learnt have proved adaptable to many different communities and contexts.

Conclusion
This evaluation is based on the responses of 38 participants of 3-day training workshops in addition to the analysis of e-mails received from participants in Peru. From this study, a number of conclusions can be drawn:

- *The workshops had a significant impact on the working practices of a number of participants in all 4 locations.*

- *A number of participants radically changed their working practices and were consistently applying theatre-based techniques across the range of their professional activity.*

- *All participants of the evaluation study introduced theatre-based exercises into their practice to some degree.*

- *There are 4 examples providing evidence of a multiplication effect. In all 4 of these examples, participants have trained colleagues, staff or professionals from related fields in the use of theatre-based techniques.*

The research suggests that the use of theatre has had a positive impact on the effectiveness of participatory development initiatives. Participants described ways in which they have used theatre-based techniques to enhance communication, generate in-depth understanding of issues and experiences and facilitate discussion of sensitive and complex issues. Theatre-based techniques facilitate a greater degree of inclusion and are accessible to all, whatever their cultural background, education, social status or gender.

These can be summarised by the words of one participant from Cajamarca:

> *The workshop allowed us to establish different forms of communication from the ones we practise every day. It let us explore our bodies, our thoughts, our emotions and even our subconscious demons. It allowed us to experience our individual and collective selves.*

ARTS-BASED RESEARCH AND EVALUATION

Julie McCarthy and Jenny Hughes[1]

In this section, we will use specific examples of exercises to present some ideas about the use of arts-based techniques for research and evaluation.

The use of arts-based exercises to research and evaluate projects can transform a task that is often seen as a necessary, dry or even dull end to a project into a dynamic, interesting and engaging experience for participants and practitioners.

The use of arts-based research techniques can mean that experiences of projects are no longer defined by the language of the evaluator – aim, objective, indicator, quantitative, qualitative – or expressed through the medium of conventional research (the written word). This language and medium can limit our understanding of impacts and present information in ways that meet the needs of external agencies rather than being relevant or useful to groups.

Through the use of image, sound, speech, movement, the body, metaphor, spatial dimension and perspective, drama and other arts present opportunities to communicate many different aspects of experience.

WHY USE THE ARTS IN RESEARCH AND EVALUATION? ARE WE JUST MAKING IT UP?
Arts-based exercises can communicate information in direct and immediate ways. They also help the research process to become more accessible to more people by increasing possibilities for participants to find a way of expressing what they want to say, in a way that suits them. Researchers need to verify information through the inclusion of multiple sources and perspectives; this process (also known as triangulation) is implicit in arts-based research with groups.

By using drama for example, groups can create visual, 3-dimensional representations of events and relationships, express what they know about them, analyse what has happened and identify the factors involved in why and how it has happened. Through 'making it up', a very detailed and informative picture of events can very quickly emerge.

So, how does this work in practice? To explore the practical applications of the arts in research and evaluation, we will employ the model of Johari's window[2].

Johari's window (Fig. 1) is a model developed in the 1960s for understanding communication in groups. The model takes the form of a 4-part window with each part representing different aspects of the ways in which knowledge exists and is communicated within groups. Johari's window demonstrates how what we know as individuals, groups or evaluators can be open to or hidden from others and from ourselves.

	Known to Self	Not Known to Self
Known to Others	1. OPEN	2. BLIND
Not Known to Others	3. HIDDEN	4. UNKNOWN

Fig. 1: Johari's window

1. The OPEN window refers to information that is freely and openly exchanged between the self and others – *common knowledge*. In the context of research and evaluation, both the individual and the group are able to analyse their experiences.

An Example: Ex. 115 Mapping Your City

In a workshop on citizenship in Callão, Peru, which involved local residents, the group was asked to map an area of the city that included many historical buildings. The aim was to discover the attitude of local residents to these places. The group mapped the area using frozen images, which were then used as a basis for improvised scenes. Through the scenes, participants articulated that local people had stopped using a playground because the local council had boarded up a nearby building and people were using it as a public toilet and a place to take drugs. This was 'common knowledge' within the group and local community.

2. The BLIND window refers to insight or understanding that is known to others, but not to the individual. In everyday interaction, others will gain this knowledge through a reading of body language, for example. In the context of research and evaluation, this window demonstrates the contrast between what the individual consciously communicates about their experiences and information that the group or the evaluator can see to be true.

The type of information produced may take the form of revelations about the impact of a project on an individual, which can be verified by further work with the individual and / or group. It is a reciprocal process, given that it is possible to comprehend something about yourself and your response to a project by how you understand other people's reactions.

An Example: Ex. 112 Image of the Word

This exercise was used with a group in Lima, Peru to research into their attitude to environmental issues. The facilitator was surprised when a group read an image that had been made of noise pollution as one of street violence. In a previous exercise, used to elicit key words relating to environmental concerns, violence had not figured. The group discovered that violence was an important issue affecting their relationship with the environment.

3. The HIDDEN window refers to knowledge that individuals hold about themselves, but which they cannot or do not share with others. This window will normally get smaller as trust builds within a group.

The idea that people hide or protect knowledge draws attention to the issue of ownership of knowledge in research and the management of powerful information. Accessing hidden information can often be done on a metaphorical or fictional level – powerful or sensitive knowledge can be expressed in stories 'owned' by groups. The use of metaphor and fiction can lead to controversial or sensitive information being revealed, providing more complex pictures of reality. This hidden knowledge might challenge the story put forward by more powerful individuals within groups and communities, drawing attention to the fact that a single community may contain many different stories about a single experience.

An Example: Ex. 119 The Inca Mural

The Inca Mural was used in a workshop with a group of young men to research into their experiences of drug use. During the exercise information was revealed which was completely new to the facilitators, even though they had been working with the group for some months. The most striking information was communicated through a story of a fictional character who joined an evangelical church to escape from a death threat. Members of the group explained that joining a church was one of the few options available to young men if they wanted to escape violence. These research findings were used to develop future work with the group.

4. The UNKNOWN window refers to knowledge that exists in groups and is beyond the awareness of both the individual and other group members. In the context of research and evaluation, this knowledge is important in terms of understanding unexpected impacts of projects, yet to be articulated by individuals. The knowledge that emerges can be challenging and highlight important new directions for practice, planning or future research.

An Example: Ex. 115 Mapping Your City

A group of Manchester University postgraduate students were involved in a consultation about their use of university facilities. They were asked to create images of areas of the campus that were most familiar to them. A striking feature of all the images created was the isolation of the key protagonist. This led to a discussion of experiences of loneliness and alienation within a university system designed for younger undergraduate students. The investigation drew attention to the social and emotional aspects of local geography, and the need to support postgraduates in both social and academic spheres.

SUMMARY

The rationale for the use of arts and drama in research is based upon the idea that knowledge is accumulated, processed and articulated in individuals and groups in ways that are both hidden and explicit.

Many research tools and approaches access information from only one or two of the quadrants of Johari's window. The examples described suggest that arts-based tools and techniques can provide access to knowledge which exists in people but is not entirely conscious or immediately available and communicable. Research needs to provide space for unexpected or hidden knowledge to evolve and emerge.

Arts-based exercises facilitate a continuous process of exploration and discussion that allow multiple representations of truth to emerge. This creative process can convey a rich and detailed picture from which to assess experience, and plan and develop future initiatives.

END NOTE
1   Jenny Hughes is an associate researcher at the Centre for Applied Theatre Research, University of Manchester
2   Luft, JT (1969) *Of Human Interaction*, Mayfield Publishing Co, Palo Alto, CA

RESOURCES FOR THEATRE AND DEVELOPMENT

The list of organisations and websites set out below is by no means exhaustive. It offers the reader access to a cross section of non-governmental organisations (NGOs), academic institutions, practitioners and networks who are all, in some way, active in the field of theatre and participatory development.

USEFUL WEBSITES

Applied and Interactive Theatre Guide
Website: http://www.tonisant.com/aitg
A resource for those who use applied theatre techniques.

The Communications Initiative
Website: http://www.comminit.com
A partnership of development organisations seeking to support advances in the effectiveness and scale of communication interventions for positive international development.

Creative Exchange
Website: http://www.creativexchange.org
International network and advocacy organisation for culture and development that collects and distributes information on projects, funding, and training, promotes best practice and lobbies for better awareness and respect of cultural rights.

Dev Media
Website: http://www.devmedia.org
Information on media for development and democracy.

One World
Website: http://www.oneworld.net
Community of over 950 NGOs working for social justice.
Excellent UK website for news on development issues around the world.

Panos Institute
Website: http://www.panos.org.uk
Panos stimulates informed and inclusive public debate around key development issues in order to foster sustainable development. It works to promote an enabling media and communications environment worldwide.

THEATRE GROUPS / DEVELOPMENT ORGANISATIONS WORKING WITH THEATRE

Active Theatre Movement
c/o T Devananth
681/2 Point Pedro Road
Nallur
Jaffna
Sri Lanka
ATM develops performance projects on a range of different issues including mine awareness.

Asociación Cultural Arte Acción

Direccion: centro cultural Loyola

Ave República del Chile 201, Colonia Palmira

Apdo 6424, Tegucigalpa

Honduras

E-mail: arteaccionhonduras@yahoo.com.mx

Arte Acción brings together artists and social scientists working to promote social inclusion and reinforce cultural identity in Honduras.

Atelier-Theatre Burkinabe (ATB)

01 B.P. 2121 Ouagadougou 01

Burkina Faso

E-mail: proskom@fasonet.bf

Burkina Faso-based organisation that integrates theatre into its many educational campaigns. Holds a biennial Theatre Festival.

Big Circle

c/o Consortium of Humanitarian Agencies

10 Kynsey Terrace

Colombo 8

Sri Lanka

Website: http://www.bigcircle.lk

A network of applied theatre practitioners working with young people and war-affected communities across Sri Lanka.

CENAP

E-mail: cenap@elogica.com.br

Website: http://www.cenap.org.br

An NGO that trains educators and social agents in the Northeast of Brazil using methodologies which incorporate theatre, writing, design, painting and dance.

Centro de Teatro do Oprimido

Av Rio Branco, 179 – 6º andar

Centro – Rio

CEP: 21140-007

Brazil

E-mail: Ctrio@domain.com.br

Website: http://www.ctorio.com.br

Brazilian centre set up by Augusto Boal – working nationally and internationally with Theatre of the Oppressed techniques.

CRIA

Maria Eugênia Viveiros Milet

Coordenadora Geral

Rua Gregório de Mattos, 21 – 1º e 2º andares

Pelourinho

Salvador-BA

Brazil

40.025-060

E-mail: Cria@allways.com.br

CRIA works to provide opportunities for young people to use theatre to speak and be heard on issues relevant to them, stimulating their participation in the construction of a more harmonious and just society.

Fundacion Crear Vale la Pena

Direccion: Bogado 571

Boulogne

Prov Buenos Aires

Argentina

E-mail: info@crearvalelapena.org.ar

Website: http://www.crearvalelapena.org.ar

This Argentinean foundation promotes the development of community cultural centres as spaces through which young, socially excluded people can receive professional artistic training, education and skills for social organisation.

La Fundación para la Investigación Teatral Kerigma

Website: http://www.uib-kerigma.colnodo.org.co

An NGO working through theatre to develop local culture and facilitate social development.

Groupe 30 Afrique

E-mail: oumarsall@hotmail.com

An African Cultural Network working to improving the circulation of cultural information for African artists and for creating connections with other cultural spaces around the world.

Grupo Cultural Yuyachkani

Jr Tacna 363, Magdalena del Mar

Lima 17

Peru

Website: http://www.pagina.de/santiago_yuyachkani

World-renowned Peruvian theatre company working in the social development field.

Yuyachkani, which translates from Quechua to mean 'I remember', is a Lima-based cultural group researching and developing work based around traditional popular celebrations, music and dance.

Grupo Teatro del Milenio

Bajada de Agua Dulce 185-c

Lima 9

Peru

E-mail: delmilenio@terra.com.pe

This theatre company researches and performs Afro-Peruvian theatre, dance and music and uses these art forms for social development work in Afro-Peruvian communities.

The Local Knowledge Activist Group

c/o S Jeyasankar

30 Old Rest House Road

Batticaloa

Sri Lanka

LKAG develops awareness about local knowledge and practices in the Eastern town of Batticaloa, including working on the reformulation of local performance using innovative approaches to participatory action research.

Centre for Development Communications
School of Community and Performing Arts
King Alfred's College
Winchester
SO22 4NR
UK
Website: http://www.cdcarts.org
Based at the School of Community and Performing Arts, CDC promotes the self-development of marginalised groups through cultural engagement and the arts.

Facultad de Ciencias y Artes de la Comunicación
Pontificia Universidad Católica del Perú
Av Universitaria Cdra 18
San Miguel, Lima 32
Peru
Website: http://www.pucp.edu.pe
University department which co-ordinates academic courses in communication for development.

Hemispheric Institute
Website: http://hemi.nyu.edu
A group of artists, academics and organisations of the Americas which is dedicated to exploring the interaction of performance and social / political life.

Institute of Development Studies
University of Sussex
Brighton
BN1 9RE
UK
Tel: +44 (0)1273 678 690
Fax: +44 (0)1273 621 202
Website: http://www.ids.ac.uk/ids
A leading centre for research and teaching on international development. Website with good resources for information on participatory development.

Nucleo de Ensino, Pesquisa e Extensao em Educacao de Jovens e Adultos e em Educacao Popular (NUPEP)
Centro De Educacao
Universidade Federal de Pernambuco
Cidade Universitaria
Recife
Pernambuco
Brazil
E-mail: nupepceufpe@bol.com.br
NUPEP is dedicated to research and practice in the field of education with young people, adolescents and adults, specifically related to questions of sustainable and integrated development and non-formal education. It is currently engaged in research on the use of the arts in literacy training and non-formal education.

O Núcleo de Estudos das Performances Afro-Ameríndias

Universidade do Rio de Janeiro

Avenida Pasteur, 296

6° andar, sala 614

Urca

Rio de Janeiro

RJ 22209-240

Brazil

Website. http://hemi.unirio.br/nepaa

Dedicated to research and exchange between cultures of African and indigenous origin, particularly their inter-relationships in Brazil. NEPAA works with performance arts and ritual.

BIBLIOGRAPHY

THEATRE AND DEVELOPMENT

Abah, Oga S (1997) *Performing Life: Case Studies in the Practice of Theatre for Development*, Shekut Books, Zaria, Nigeria

Banham, M, Gibbs, J and Osfisan, F (1999) *African Theatre in Development*, James Currey, Oxford

Boon, R and Plastow, J (1998) *Theatre Matters: Performance and Culture on the World Stage*, Cambridge University Press, Cambridge

Byam, L Dale (1999) *Community in Motion: Theatre for Development in Africa*, Bergin and Garvey, London

Cohen-Cruz, J (ed) (1998) *Radical Street Performance: An International Anthology*, London, Routledge

Epskamp, KP (1989) *Theatre in Search of Social Change*, Ceso, The Hague

Frank, M (1995) *Theatre in the Service of Health Education*, Bayreuth African Studies, Bayreuth

Haedicke, SC and Nelhaus, T (eds) (2001) *Performing Democracy: International Perspectives on Urban Community-Based Performance*, The University of Michigan Press, Michigan

Jackson, T (ed) (1994) *Learning Through Theatre, New Perspectives on Theatre in Education*, Routledge, London

Kaliba, S and Breitinger, E (1994) *Theatre for Development*, Bayreuth, Rossdorf

Kidd, R (1982) *The Popular Performing Arts, Non-Formal Education, and Social Change*, Ceso, The Hague

Kidd, R (1984) *From People's Theatre for Revolution to Popular Theatre for Reconstruction*, Ceso, The Hague

Liebmann, M (ed) (1999) *Arts Approaches to Conflict*, Jessica Kingsley Publishers, London

MacDougall, J (1998) *Contaminating Theatre*, Northwestern University Press, Evanston, Illinois

MDA, Z (1983) *When People Play People: Development Communication through Theatre*, Zed Books, London

Mlama, PM (1991) *Culture and Development: The Popular Theatre Approach in Africa*, The Nordic Africa Institute, Uppsala

Prentki, T and Selman, J (2003) *Popular Theatre and Political Culture*, Intellect, Exeter

Sahli, K (ed) (1998) *African Theatre for Development: Art for Self-determination*, Intellect, Exeter

Schutzman, M and Cohen-Cruz, J (1994) *Playing Boal: Theatre, Therapy, Activism*, Routledge, London

Srampickal, J (1995) *Voice to the Voiceless: The Power of People's Theatre in India*, C Hurst & Co, London

Taylor, P (2003) *Applied Theatre, Creating Transformative Encounters in the Community*, Heinemann, Portsmouth, NH

Thompson, J (2003) *Applied Theatre: Bewilderment and Beyond*, Peter Lang, Oxford

THEATRE GAMES AND EXERCISES

Boal, A (1970) *Theatre of the Oppressed*, Pluto Press, London

Boal, A (1992) *Games for Actors and Non-Actors*, Routledge, London

Boal, A (1995) *The Rainbow of Desire*, Routledge, London

Boal, A (1998) *Legislative Theatre*, Routledge, London

Brandes, D and Phillips, H (1979) *The Gamester's Handbook 1*, Nelson Thornes, Cheltenham

Brandes, D and Phillips, H (1982) *The Gamester's Handbook 2*, Nelson Thornes, Cheltenham

Brandes, D and Norris, N (1998) *The Gamester's Handbook 3*, Nelson Thornes, Cheltenham

Jennings, S (1986) *Creative Drama in Group Work*, Winslow Press, Bicester

Johnston, C (1998) *House Of Games*, Nick Hern Books, London

Johnstone, K (1991) *Impro*, Routledge, London

Koppett, K (2001) *Training to Imagine: Practical Improvisational Theatre Techniques to Enhance Creativity, Teamwork, Leadership, and Learning*, Stylus, LLC, Sterling, VA

Macbeth, F and Fine, N (1992) *Playing with Fire*, New Society, Philadelphia

Poulter, C (1987) *Playing The Game 1*, Macmillan, London

Rosenberg, H (1987) *Creative Drama and Imagination: Transforming Ideas into Action*, Holt, Reinhart and Winston, New York

Spolin, V (1983) *Improvisation for the Theatre*, Northwestern University Press, Evanston

Spolin, V (1986) *Theatre Games for the Classroom*, Northwestern University Press, Evanston

PARTICIPATORY DEVELOPMENT

Arevalo, M and Guijt, I (1998) *Participatory Monitoring and Evaluation*, IIED, London

Burkey, S (ed) (1993) *People First: A Guide to Self-reliant Participatory Rural Development*, Zed Books, London

Carmen, R (1996) *Autonomous Development*, Zed Books, London

Chambers, R (1997) *Whose Reality Counts? Putting the First Last*, ITDG Publishing, London

Chambers, R (2002) *Participatory Workshops: A Sourcebook of 21 Sets of Ideas and Activities*, Earthscan, London

Craig, G and Mayo, M (eds) (1995) *Community Empowerment*, Zed Books, London

Eade, D (1997) *Capacity Building: An Approach to People-Centred Development*, Oxfam, Oxford

Fals Borda, O (1998) *People's Participation: Challenges Ahead*, ITDG Publishing, London

Freire, P (1972) *Cultural Action for Freedom*, Penguin, Harmondsworth

Freire, P (1972) *Pedagogy of The Oppressed*, Penguin, Harmondsworth

Friedman, J (1992) *Empowerment*, Blackwell, Cambridge, MA

Gajanayake, S and Gajanayake, J (1993) *Community Empowerment: A Participatory Training Manual on Community Project Development*, Office of International Training and Consultation, Illinois

Guijt, I and Haul Shah, M (1998) *The Myth of Community: Gender Issues in Participatory Development*, ITDG Publishing, London

Kaufman, M and Alfonso, HD (eds) (1997) *Community Power and Grassroots Democracy: The Transformation of Social Life*, Zed Books, London

Kleymeyer, C (ed) (1986) *Cultural Expression and Grassroots Development*, Lynne Rienner Publishers, London

Lovett, T (ed) (1988) *Radical Approaches to Adult Education: A Reader*, Croom Helm, London

Lovett, T, Clarke, C and Kilmurray, A (1983) *Adult Education and Community Action: Adult Education and Popular Social Movements*, Croom Helm, London

Nelson, N and Wright, S (1995) *Power and Participatory Development: Theory and Practice*, Intermediate Technology, London

Nyerere, J (1973) *Freedom and Development*, Oxford University Press, Oxford

Pieterse, N and Parekh, B (1995) *The Decolonisation of the Imagination*, Zed Books, London

Rhamen, MA (1993) *People's Self Development: Perspectives on Participatory Action Research*, Zed Books, London

Taylor, P (1993) *The Texts of Paulo Freire*, Open University Press, Buckingham

Verhelst, T (1990) *No Life Without Roots*, Zed Books, London

Walters, S and Manicom, L (eds) (1996) *Gender in Popular Education*, Zed Books, London